OSPREY
PUBLISHING

German Seaman 1939–45

Gordon Williamson · Illustrated by John White

First published in Great Britain in 2001 by Osprey Publishing, Elms Court, Chapel Way, Botley, Oxford OX2 9LP, United Kingdom. Email: info@ospreypublishing.com

ISBN 1 84176 327 6

Editor: Simone Drinkwater
Design: Ken Vail Graphic Design, Cambridge, UK
Index by Alan Rutter
Originated by Magnet Harlequin, Uxbridge, UK
Printed in China through World Print Ltd.

FOR A CATALOGUE OF ALL BOOKS PUBLISHED BY OSPREY MILITARY AND AVIATION PLEASE CONTACT:

The Marketing Manager, Osprey Direct USA,
c/o Motorbooks International, PO Box 1,
Osceola, WI 54020-0001, USA.
Email: info@ospreydirectusa.com

The Marketing Manager, Osprey Direct UK, PO Box 140,
Wellingborough, Northants, NN8 4ZA, United Kingdom.
Email: info@ospreydirect.co.uk

www.ospreypublishing.com

Artist's note

Readers may care to note that the original paintings from which the colour plates in this book were prepared are available for private sale. All reproduction copyright whatsoever is retained by the Publishers. All enquiries should be addressed to:

John White, 5107 C Monroe Road, Charlotte, NC 28205, United States of America

The Publishers regret that they can enter into no correspondence upon this matter.

FRONT COVER **Three junior naval ratings pose for a group photograph on board their Minesweeper in this pre-war photograph. The sailor on the left is Jakob Mallmann, who lost his life serving as Stabsobermaschinist (Engine Room 'Chief') on U-377 on his 13th war cruise, when the boat was believed to have been hit by one of its own faulty torpedoes.**

CONTENTS

GERMAN SEAMAN 1939–45

INTRODUCTION

Unlike the Royal Navy, the German Navy had only a relatively short history by the outbreak of the Second World War in 1939. Despite this, a strong sense of tradition and honour had been engendered, and, most importantly, a record of few actual defeats in naval actions.

Of all branches of the military and paramilitary services of the Third Reich, the Kriegsmarine was by far the least politically indoctrinated. Though there were no doubt many convinced supporters of National Socialism within its ranks, the Navy was a traditional, conservative organisation, that kept its distance from politics as far as was possible in the Third Reich. Hitler himself is quoted as saying, 'I have a reactionary Army, a National Socialist Air Force and a Christian Navy.'

Despite the fierce competition that developed between Great Britain and Germany as Kaiser Wilhelm strove to challenge Britain's control of the seas, the seamen of both countries retained a high degree of respect for each other. This most certainly continued into WWII during which

A favourite past-time of many servicemen – drinks and a sing-song in the mess. This rather looks like an all-services *Soldatenheim*, or soldiers club, rather than a naval mess, as there are a number of Army and Airforce personnel in the background. Most of those present are junior ranks, with only a handful of NCOs present.

the war at sea was fought in a much more chivalrous fashion than was the war on land. With only rare exceptions on both sides, sailors tended to see the sea itself as the greatest enemy, made the best efforts they could to rescue shipwrecked enemy sailors and gave full credit to the gallantry shown by the enemy in battle.

The respect accorded to the men of the Kriegsmarine by their adversaries can be gauged by incidences such as the dropping of a wreath by HMS *Duke of York* over the spot at which the battlecruiser *Scharnhorst* was sunk. The British commanding admiral was quoted as saying 'I hope that if any of you are called upon to lead a ship into action against an opponent many times superior, you will command your ship as gallantly as the *Scharnhorst* was commanded.'

The plaque placed by Merseyside Submarine Old Comrades Association at the U-boat memorial at Laboe, near Kiel, sums up the almost universal feeling of combat sailors of most nations towards each other. It simply states, 'Men who served the sea were not enemies, but opponents.'

CHRONOLOGY

1848	The first German Navy is formed during the war with Denmark to oppose the Danish blockade of German waters.
1852	The Navy is disbanded and its ships pass to Prussia where they are used principally as a transport force for the Army.
1853	The Prussian Admiralty is formed.
1866	The Navy of the North German Federation (the first Bundesmarine) is formed.
1871	Following the successful conclusion of the Franco-Prussian War and the unification of the German states under Prussia, the Imperial German Navy is formed (Kaiserliche Marine).
1916	Battle of Jutland: the Navy's first major engagement resulted in a 'draw' with the vastly more powerful Royal Navy.
21 June 1919	High Seas Fleet scuttled at Scapa Flow.
1 January 1921	Formation of the emasculated Reichsmarine.
19 May 1931	Launch of the *Deutschland*, first of the 'pocket battleships'.
21 May 1935	Foundation of the Kriegsmarine.
3 October 1936	Launch of the battlecruiser *Scharnhorst*.
8 December 1938	Launch of the aircraft carrier *Graf Zeppelin*.
14 February 1939	Launch of battleship *Bismarck*.
28 April 1939	Hitler renounces the Anglo-German Naval Agreement.
13 September 1939	Sinking of the *Royal Oak* at Scapa Flow by U-47.
23 November 1939	British auxiliary cruiser *Rawalpindi* sunk by *Scharnhorst*.
17 December 1939	Scuttling of the pocket battleship *Admiral Graf Spee*.
31 March 1940	Auxiliary cruiser *Atlantis* sets off on what was to become an immensely successful war cruise.
9 April 1940	Heavy cruiser *Blücher* sunk in Oslo Fjord.
24 May 1941	Battlecruiser HMS *Hood* sunk by the *Bismarck*.
27 May 1941	*Bismarck* sunk by British task force.
14 November 1941	Aircraft carrier *Ark Royal* sunk by U-81.
25 November 1941	Battleship *Barham* sunk by U-331.
12–13 February 1942	The 'Channel dash'. *Gneisenau*, *Scharnhorst* and *Prinz Eugen* pass safely through the English Channel under the nose of the Royal Navy.
5 July 1942	Combined navy/airforce attack decimates Convoy PQ17.
26 December 1943	Battle of the North Cape. *Scharnhorst* sunk by British task force.
12 November 1944	*Tirpitz* sunk by RAF bombers at her moorings in Norway.

29 January 1945	*Prinz Eugen* bombards Soviet troops near Gotenhafen.
30 January 1945	*Admiral Hipper* assists in evacuating 1,700 civilians from Gotenhafen as the Red Army nears.
2 February 1945	*Admiral Hipper* bombed and sunk in dock at Kiel.
8 February 1945	*Lützow* bombards Soviet troops movements near Frauenburg-Elbing.
8 March 1945	*Admiral Scheer* evacuates refugees from Gotenhafen.
10–15 March 1945	*Admiral Scheer* bombards Soviet troop movements near Kolberg.
30 March 1945	*Prinz Eugen* in action against Soviet land forces near Oxhoft.
9 April 1945	*Admiral Scheer*, damaged by near misses in bombing raid on Kiel, capsizes.
13 April 1945	*Lützow* severely damaged by near misses during bombing raid on Swinemünde; immobilised but guns continue to be used to bombard approaching Soviet forces until scuttled in early May.
20 April 1945	Out of ammunition, *Prinz Eugen* puts into port at Copenhagen, where she remains until the end of the war, the last surviving heavy unit of the Kriegsmarine.

RECRUITMENT

The period following WWI was, for Germany, a time of great misery, with catastrophic levels of unemployment and rampant inflation, made worse by the burden of unrealistic reparation payments to its former enemies. Germany found itself permitted only a minuscule navy, equipped with small coastal vessels such as minesweepers, torpedo boats and a few obsolete dreadnaught battleships. Reduced to a mere 15,000 men, the Navy retained only those whom it considered the best and most experienced. The Navy was permitted only minimal recruitment and could afford to be extremely choosy, considering the huge pool of manpower to pick from.

With the rise to power of the National Socialists and Hitler's eventual return to conscription and compulsory military service for all, the Navy remained the smallest of the armed forces and continued its policy of picking only the best recruits.

The basic requirements were that the potential naval recruit was at least 17 years of age and under 23. He had to be both mentally and physically fit (including the provision that he must have good teeth), be of German nationality, have no criminal record, be in possession of a satisfactory school leaving certificate and have completed compulsory service with the *Reichsarbeitsdienst*, or State Labour Service. Those who were part way through an apprenticeship would be expected to complete it before enlisting and those under the age of 21 would require parental consent. The Navy made it quite clear that they were particularly interested in recruiting men with a skilled trade such as mechanics, electricians, etc. Certainly the extremely high unemployment rates in the late 1920s and early 1930s gave the Navy every opportunity to be selective in whom they accepted.

Provided he fulfilled these basic conditions, the prospective sailor would make a written application in his own hand (interestingly, there were no application forms as such – each applicant simply had to draft up his own style of application), with full personal details, covering obvious items such as name, address, date and place of birth, religion, height, weight, educational accomplishments and any employment history. In addition, details were to be given of sporting abilities and achievements, whether or not a driving licence was held, any *Reichsarbeitsdienst* service, membership of the Party (or Hitler Youth for younger applicants), technical skills and any foreign languages spoken.

The prospective applicant would then visit his local police station and ask for a Volunteer Certificate. This confirmed that he had no criminal convictions, and that the rest of the personal information he had given had been verified from official documents.

Finally, the applicant would obtain two passport photographs in civilian clothing and post them along with his application and Volunteer Certificate to the office of the Second Admiral of the Nordsee (North Sea) or Ostsee (Baltic). All of this had to be done at least one full year before the intended date of enlistment.

The next stage in enlistment would be the receipt by the applicant of an enlistment questionnaire and instructions to attend a local doctor's surgery for a medical inspection. Assuming the medical examination was passed and the answers given in the questionnaire were acceptable, the applicant would receive an Acceptance Form instructing him to report to the offices of the local *Wehrkreis* (Military District Offices). Here he would face yet another, final, medical and the requisite forms would be filled in and signed to complete the enlistment. A minimum service period of 4 years (not including a 12-month training period) was required, with a 12-year minimum requirement for those who wished to serve as NCOs. The new recruit would then be issued a *Wehrpass* (Military Pass), which included his photograph in civilian clothing, his address and all personal details including those of his inducting unit. Having received this pass, the recruit would return home to await his call-up notice instructing him to report to his unit.

Although recruits could volunteer for any branch of the armed services, much would depend on the recruiting team at their local *Wehrkreis* offices, especially during wartime. One acquaintance of the author, who came from an engineering background and had served in the *Marine Hitler Jugend* obtaining qualifications in wireless telegraphy, was keen to join the Navy, and indeed seemed an ideal candidate, but was foiled by an obstructive administration officer who was himself a member of the Luftwaffe's anti-aircraft branch. Frustrated by this officer's attempts to enlist him into the

Original recruiting pamphlet for the Kriegsmarine. Entitled 'How do I join the Navy?', it gave the prospective recruit full details of the enlistment process and showed photos of sailors in training. These publications are now sought-after collector's items.

Wie komme ich zur Kriegsmarine

Ein Merkheft für Freiwillige (Kriegsausgabe)

Sailors of the Kriegsmarine parade through the streets of Berlin in a ceremony to celebrate the battle of Jutland. Parades such as these kept the Navy in the public's eye and certainly helped recruitment.

Air Force, he made a disparaging remark about the flak and immediately found himself allocated to the Army as an infantryman. In the event, he became a war hero and holder of the coveted Knight's Cross of the Iron Cross for gallantry on the Eastern Front.

Ultimately, the recruit would receive a telegram instructing him to report to his unit for military service on a set date and time.

Recruits to the Navy came from all over Germany, and not just the coastal areas where there already was an established seafaring tradition. It is almost certain that an element of attraction of the Navy was to avoid what might have been perceived as much tougher service in the Army. Many of those who applied to join the Navy were former merchant seamen who had been laid off as their employers cut back on costs during the great depression. Recruiting the best men from this source gave the Navy the opportunity to take on men who were already experienced sailors. Some of the best-known U-boat aces, for example, were former Merchant Navy sailors.

The Navy, like the German Army, was generally perceived as having been unbeaten in battle in the First World War. The battle of Jutland was effectively a draw, therefore the German Navy had never suffered a comprehensive defeat. On the other hand, exploits of ships such as the *Goeben* and the *Emden* against overwhelming odds, and the dramatic successes of the U-boats, had gained the Navy an excellent reputation for skill, bravery and honour. The scuttling of the High Seas Fleet at Scapa Flow in 1919 had been considered the honourable thing to do, to prevent German ships being ignominiously handed over to the Allies.

The punitive terms of the Treaty of Versailles left the German Navy emasculated. With nothing left but a few obsolete torpedo boats and battleships, the Germans were forced to recreate their navy from scratch. This resulted in a small force, but one equipped with the most modern and technically advanced ships in the world.

The Navy, therefore, had no trouble recruiting eager young men anxious to serve. Recruitment teams travelled to every corner of the Reich to enrol the cream of available manpower. The recruiting posters of the day concentrated on powerful imagery such as battleships firing salvos from their main armament or on the sleek U-boats, the grey wolves of the sea.

The already high profile of the Kriegsmarine was considerably boosted by the sinking of the battleship *Royal Oak* at Scapa Flow, the very place where the High Seas Fleet had been scuttled twenty years earlier, by Günther Prien in U-47. Prien and his crew were summoned to the Chancellory in Berlin, where every man was decorated, and dined with Adolf Hitler. The fullest possible publicity was given to the event, and huge crowds gathered to greet the conquering hero and his crew. The standing of the Navy in the eyes of the German public could scarcely have been higher. Magazines, such as the famed *Signal*, regularly contained articles with full-colour pictures of naval personnel in action, and the Navy itself published its own magazine *Die Kriegsmarine*. It is difficult to imagine what more could have been done to promote recruitment into the Navy, and there was certainly no shortage of applicants.

The elements of selection used by the Navy ensured that those who were inducted generally were suitable for the task, and it has been estimated that drop-out rates during training were reduced by up to 40 per cent through the application of much tougher initial selection procedures.

Once the war began, and the need to make up manpower losses became increasingly important, some of the more stringent recruitment criteria were quietly dropped. It would no longer be necessary, for example, for a prospective sailor to have a perfect set of teeth. The country could no longer afford the luxury of quite such a high degree of selectivity. Standards, however, did remain very high, especially for sea-going personnel. As the Navy expanded, more and more men were required to fill a variety of different positions. Not only were sailors required, but naval administrative staff, musicians, naval fortification engineers, judicial staff, naval police, civilian auxiliaries, chaplains, etc. Many of these administrative positions were looked on with some disdain by sea-going personnel. Administrative staff wore naval uniforms but with silver rather than gold insignia, earning the perjorative name *Silberlings*.

The recruitment of personnel from outside the Reich also became common, to include actual non-Germans as well as ethnic Germans. The most extreme example of this was the recruitment into the Kriegsmarine of a Croat Naval Legion, some 900 strong, in the summer of 1941. This unit was commanded by a Croat officer, Andre Vrkljana, who was given a commission as a Fregattenkapitän in the German Navy.

A group of recruits swear their oath to the flag at a special ceremony. The recruits actually taking the oath may be seen at the opposite end of the hall, standing in front of the Reichskriegsflagge.

The unit even gained some turncoat Ukrainians who deserted from the Soviet Navy, and was expanded in 1943 with the addition of a battery of coastal artillery. These Croats in German uniform served in the Black Sea area until eventually absorbed into the Croat Navy in 1944.

Once enlisted, the typical naval recruit had no choice in the trade he would follow, this being decided by the Navy, based on the abilities and skills he held. For instance, someone with acute hearing, clear handwriting and some electronic skills would make a good candidate for radio operator. A number of career paths, or *Laufbahn*, existed, these being as follows:

Laufbahn I	Seaman Career
Laufbahn II	Machinist Career (Engine Room Personnel)
Laufbahn III	Helmsman/Navigator Career
Laufbahn IV	Radio Operator Career
Laufbahn V	Carpenter Career
Laufbahn VI	Ordnance Career
Laufbahn VII	Mechanic Career (Artificers)
Laufbahn VIII	Unused
Laufbahn IX	Administrative Career
Laufbahn X	Clerical Career
Laufbahn XI	Medical Orderly Career
Laufbahn XII	Musician Career
Laufbahn XIV	Coastal Artillery Career
Laufbahn XV	Motor Transport Career

An original service contract for a naval officer, the nineteen-year-old Emmerich, Baron von Mirbach. Note that as an officer, he has signed on to serve for *unbegrenzte Zeit* – an unlimited period of time, with the Baltic Fleet. He has been accepted into 2 Schiffsstammabteilung at Stralsund to begin his training. Baron von Mirbach successfully completed his training and became an engineering officer, ultimately joining the U-boat service. He survived the war.

Approximately 50 per cent of each ship's crew (from U-boat to battleship) were from the Seaman Career, the remainder being a mix of the specialist trades.

In 1941, the Navy also began to recruit youths of 14–15 years into special preparatory schools to train them for service as future naval NCOs once they had reached the age of 17.

In addition to all of the other criteria previously mentioned, potential officers had to complete their written submissions in the archaic *Sütterlin* handwriting script, which was almost impossible for non-Germans (and even many Germans) to read. So difficult was this script to decipher that it is said the Allies prohibited it at the end of the war for fear that it would be used to pass secret messages. Officer applications also had to provide information not only on the applicant himself, but also on his parents, grandparents, sisters and brothers and the reason for wishing to serve as an officer. A family tree stretching back at least three generations had also to be provided along with the names of three male referees and the written permission of the applicant's father.

The Navy was seen as a very honourable profession, and unattached naval officers, in their elegant uniforms, were seen as prime candidates to be husbands by mothers of young women from the best families. The life of career naval officers, however, was no easy one, as the training they were about to face was some of the toughest, both physically and academically, of any of the services.

The imposing edifice of the Marineschule Mürwick, with its Gothic architecture, serves the German Navy to this day.

TRAINING

Once enlisted, and the sailor had joined his unit to commence training, his *Wehrpass* would be taken from him. It would follow him throughout his military career, not held by him personally, but in his unit office. In its place, he would be issued a *Soldbuch* (paybook) that doubled as his personal identity document, and contained a photograph of the sailor. It also recorded any kit issued, pay and pay supplements, inoculations, medical treatment, the details of his ID disc, promotions and awards or decorations earned. One thing that the *Soldbuch* did not record was training, though all courses and training establishments attended continued to be recorded in the *Wehrpass*.

The sailor's pools for the German Navy came under the command of the Second Admiral of the North Sea or Baltic commands (*2. Admiral der Nordsee* or *Ostsee*). All sailors were allocated to one of the two main naval commands, the North Sea or Baltic, and were posted to the appropriate *Schiffsstammdivision* (sailor's pool). Wartime expansion and reorganisation saw this structure change from the basic division into six regiments (three each in the Baltic and North Sea commands) with further subdivisions into a final total of 31 training detachments (the *Schiffsstammabteilung*) where sailors carried out their initial basic training. (The numbering sequence ran up to 32, but Detachment 29 was never made operational). These were based at the following locations:

Kiel (Ostsee) Schiffsstammabteilungen 1 and 3
Wilhelmshaven (Nordsee) Schiffsstammabteilungen 2, 4 and 6
Eckernförde (Ostsee) Schiffsstammabteilung 5
Stralsund (Ostsee) Schiffsstammabteilungen 7, 9 (for NCO Training), 11 (for NCO Training) and 32
Leer (Nordsee) Schiffsstammabteilung 8
Wesermünde (Nordsee) Schiffsstammabteilung 10 (NCO Training)
Brake (Nordsee) Schiffsstammabteilung 12 (NCO Training)
Sassnitz (Ostsee) Schiffsstammabetilung 13
Glückstadt (Nordsee) Schiffsstammabteilung 14
Beverloo in Belgium (Nordsee) Schiffsstammabteilungen 15 (NCO Training) and 22
Bergen in Norway (Nordsee) Schiffsstammabteilung 16
Memel (Ostsee) Schiffsstammabteilung 17
Buxtehude (Nordsee) Schiffsstammabteilung 18
Diedenhofen (Ostsee) Schiffsstammabteilung 19
Norden (Nordsee) Schiffsstammabteilung 20
Leba (Ostsee) Schiffsstammabteilung 21
Deutsche-Krone (Ostsee) Schiffsstammabteilung 23 (Naval Artillery)
Groningen in Holland (Nordsee) Schiffsstammabteilung 24 (Naval Artillery)
Pillau (Ostsee) Schiffsstammabteilung 25 (Naval Artillery)
Wazep (Nordsee) Schiffsstammabteilung 26
Ollerup in Denmark (Ostsee) Schiffsstammabteilung 27 (Naval Artillery)
Sennheim (Nordsee) Schiffsstammabteilung 28 (for foreign volunteers)
Wittmund (Nordsee) Schiffsstammabteilung 30
Windau (Ostsee) Schiffsstammabteilung 31

Initial basic training for sailors consisted of the same common military syllabus through which Army infantry soldiers were processed. All sailors had to don field grey uniform and participate in drill exercises, exhaustive physical training, assault courses, gunnery and bayonet practice, route marches and the general range of whatever delights might be dreamed up by their training NCOs.

Once deemed fit to pass out as soldiers (the German custom is to refer to all servicemen as 'Soldiers', whether from the Army, Air Force or Navy), the recruits would pass to specialist training schools that would teach them the trade relative to the *Laufbahn* to which they had been allocated. Some of the major training schools included:

Marinenachrichtenschule Naval Signals School, at Mürwick and Aurich
Sperrschule Naval Defences School, at Kiel

Marinesanitätsschule	Navy Medical School, at Kiel
Torpedoschule	Torpedo School, at Mürwick
Schiffsartillerieschule	Ships Artillery School, at Kiel
Kustenartillerieschule	Coastal Artillery School, at Swinemünde
Steuermannsschule	Helmsman/Navigator School, at Mürwick
Marineflugabwehrschule	Navy Anti-Aircraft Defence School, at Swinemünde
Marinesportschule	Navy Sports School (for PT Instructors), at Mürwick
Marinegasschutzschule	Navy Gas Defence School, at Kiel

NCOs

After the reintroduction of conscription, vast increases in NCO grades required put the training establishments under considerable strain. The existing NCO school at Friedrichsort could not cope with the influx, so a new, second NCO training school was opened at Wesermünde (Bremerhaven), the two becoming known as *Marineunteroffizierlehrabteilung 1* and *2*. In 1938, a new purpose-built NCO training school was opened at Plön, which exists to this day. Unlike officers, who could apply to join the Navy as such, NCOs were chosen by selection from the ranks. Their own officers kept a close eye on high-quality sailors with several years experience to identify suitable future NCOs.

Indeed, the practice of promoting NCOs from the ranks was not new, but the old procedure of simply promoting a senior rating who had given good service and leaving him to acquire gradually the skills of the higher rank had proven far from satisfactory. The difference with the new system was that once selected, the new NCO would be required to sign on for a spell of at least 12 years service, and was then put through extensive professional training to ensure that he would have all the skills needed as an NCO. This meant that by the time a sailor was selected, he was already highly experienced, fit, and well motivated.

Once selected, he would be sent for advanced technical training for the trade relevant to his *Laufbahn*, and this could take anything from three to ten months, before moving on to NCO school. At NCO school, he would once again don field grey, and go through further intensive training, both on the drill square and in simulated combat training where he would gain the confidence required to give clear, concise, well thought out orders under all sorts of adverse conditions. Given all this, as well as the advanced technical specialisation skills

Sailors on the training ground, with a heavy machine gun. Training units were often equipped with obsolete or obsolescent weapons, such as the MG08 shown here with the distinctive water-cooled jacket over the barrel. So little did naval uniforms change after the First World War that this may have passed for a photo from a much earlier time; but on the original print the eagle and swastika emblem of the Third Reich can be clearly seen above the national colours cockade on the cap of the instructor on the right.

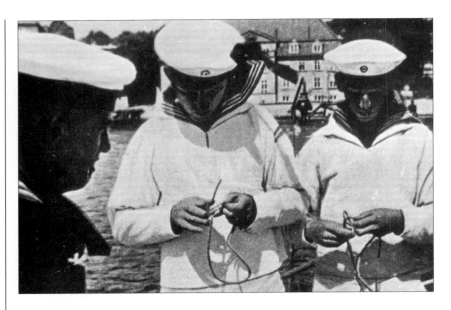

Two recruits practise one of the traditional skills of a sailor – tying knots. Just visible on the original print are the gothic script letters of the ship's tally ribbons worn by these sailors, indicating the photo was taken after the change from block script in 1929. The lack of the eagle and swastika national emblem on the shirt and cap indicates a date before 1935, suggesting that this photo was taken sometime in the early 1930s.

of his *Laufbahn*, there were few NCOs in any other branch of the armed services with such a high multi-skill level as those of the Kriegsmarine.

Officers

The initial part of officer training was common to all branches, before splitting into various specialist training paths. Line officers had the suffix '*zur See*' appended to their rank, engineer ranks were followed by the abbreviation (*Ing.*), for *Ingenieur*, weapons officers ranks were followed by the letter (*W*), for *Waffen-offizier* and administrative staff by (*V*) for *Verwaltung*.

The initial training was as follows:

Induction and basic training	5 months
Practical training	4 months (Sail training for line officers, workshop training for engineers or weapons officers)
Promotion to Cadet	
Service on a training ship	9 months
Examinations	followed by promotion to Fähnrich
Home leave	15 days

Thereafter, more specialised training commenced. (Mürwick refers to Marineschule Mürwick, the premier German Naval Academy), as below:

Line Officers	Engineer	Gunnery
Mürwick 7 months	Mürwick 7 months	Ships Artillery School 6 months
Weapons 5 months	Engineer exams	Shipyard 6 months
Fleet service 6 months	Workshop 5 months	Mürwick 7 months
Promotion to Leutnant zur See	Fleet service 6 months	Weapons 5 months
	Promotion to Leutnant (Ing)	Fleet service 6 months
		Promotion to Leutnant (W)

It can be seen that there were several common elements even in the second part of training, but these were interspersed with more role-specific training.

Officer training began at Danholm on the Baltic, where they were put through a two-day induction course comprised almost entirely of extremely strenuous physical training and interviews which would weed out one in every four applicants. Those who passed were issued uniforms and allowed to continue training. At each stage of training, it was official policy to mix recruits continuously so that they did not always work alongside friends they had made and that cliques therefore would not be formed.

The training itself was extremely arduous, with the training NCOs putting the potential officers through the mill. Unscheduled route marches could be sprung on the trainees any time of the day or night. Kit and uniform inspections found fault with the slightest imperfection, and those unfortunate enough to be found wanting would be given extra fatigue duties or drill exercises during what should have been free time. The inevitable 'show parades', known and hated by soldiers the world over, could involve cadets struggling on to the parade square carrying the steel locker cabinets from their quarters to show their instructor that everything inside was spick and span, then having to stagger back and replace the locker and rush back to the parade square, all within a few minutes. Failure to get back in time resulted in even more fatigues.

Recruits were chased around the drill square in full combat kit with heavy pack, steel helmet and wearing gas marks, all at double time, until they were ready to drop from sheer exhaustion. At Mürwick, there is apparently a sandy headland which ends in a precipitously steep slope running down to the water's edge. Recruits were chased headlong down the slope to the water's edge, only to have to turn around and run up the slope again, in full battle kit and often wearing gas marks, until they were almost in a state of collapse.

Whatever might be felt about officers by the lower ranks, it must be said that the physical aspects of their training were every bit as hard as, if not harder than, that suffered by lower grades.

Naval officers did their shipboard training on sail trainers, the best known of which is probably the *Gorch Fock*. This was extremely tough training before the mast, and deaths in training were not unknown, the training weeding out those who did not possess the required determination, physical ability and strength of character. This exhausting training was generally followed (in peacetime at least) by a goodwill cruise into foreign waters aboard a major surface warship. This was also very hard work, but gave many young officers their first chance to see the world. Tough examinations, followed by promotion to Officer Cadet for those who passed, would in turn be followed by a welcome two-week leave. Thereafter, training would differ depending on the career path the cadet wished to follow, but one common feature was the obligatory seven-month course at Marineschule Mürwick, the most famous of all the German naval academies, located in a hugely

This photograph shows a Seekadet in rather formal dress with winged collar and black bow tie. His cap is the type worn by warrant officers as well as officer cadets/officer aspirants. His status of Seekadet is indicated by the gold star with oval border worn on the left upper arm.

LEFT **All officer trainees were obliged to complete a period of service on a sail training ship. This photograph shows the *Gorch Fock*. Note that her cadets are all aloft manning the spars, a task requiring a good sense of balance and strong nerves even in calm waters such as here.**

BELOW **A group of chief petty officers in the classroom at engineering school. The engineer CPO's combined rank/trade patch of a cogwheel superimposed upon a fouled anchor, all over a single chevron, can be clearly seen on the sleeve of the man in the centre of the front row. (Jak P. Mallmann Showell)**

impressive Gothic-style building built near Flensburg on the orders of Kaiser Wilhelm II and first opened in November 1910.

Due to the high degree of technical specialisation within the Navy, most ranks had some form of advance training, certainly more so than in the other branches of the armed forces. By the latter part of the war, however, the Kriegsmarine, with the exception of the U-boats, was a spent force. Most capital ships had been destroyed. In the cases of some, like the *Tirpitz*, their purpose lay in providing a threat which required the enemy to tie down considerable forces to guard against her putting to sea. Others, like the *Prinz Eugen* and *Admiral Scheer*, were used in last-ditch support actions, bombarding Soviet targets on land to cover the retreat of the German Army and the evacuation of civilians.

Many experienced and highly trained sailors, including U-boat crews, were transferred to the Army or Waffen-SS, or were thrown into the Kriegsmarine's own infantry units formed in the closing months of the war. The 'conversion training' for infantry duties was rudimentary to say the least. One former U-boat crewman commented that he received but one day's infantry 'refresher' training, one day being instructed on how to use the Panzerfaust anti-tank weapon, and one day on small-arms training. On the fourth day, he was in action against British armoured units near Hamburg. Unsurprisingly, losses were heavy, though the former sailors did give a good account of themselves. A recent detractor of Grossadmiral Dönitz criticised this 'desperate idea', but the fact remains that these Navy tank hunters destroyed over 40 armoured vehicles in just two days of fighting between 18 and 20 April, halting a British offensive in their sector. So, although the conversion training was less than intensive, the quality of the men themselves showed through.

A signals trainee undergoing instruction at the naval signals school at Mürwick. He is wearing parade uniform (identifiable by the collar of the shirt being worn outside the jacket – the collar being worn inside with the pea jacket). His cap carries the *Marinenachrichtenschule Mürwick* ribbon.
(Jak P. Mallmann Showell)

APPEARANCE

Naval clothing worn by the Kriegsmarine is a huge study in its own right and in-depth coverage is outside the scope of this book. For those who wish to study the subject in greater depth, a number of useful works are listed in the bibliography. Before describing some of the forms of dress worn by the typical Kriegsmarine seaman, some basic comments, which apply to all forms of dress, may help to avoid repetition.

After 1935, all forms of tunic, jacket, or shirt carried the national emblem of an eagle with outspread wings clutching a wreathed swastika on the left breast. This was generally in yellow thread or gold wire on dark blue for normal clothing, blue on white for summer dress, yellow

ABOVE LEFT **This interesting photograph shows Merchant Navy Captain Otto Giese after his voluntary transfer to U-boats, whereupon he had to revert to the ranks and prove himself before regaining officer status. On his left breast, as well as the U-boat War Badge, is the Blockade Breaker Badge, awarded for his part in returning the merchantman *Anneliese Essberger* through the Allied blockade to Germany. (Otto Giese)**

ABOVE RIGHT **Three petty officers in normal service dress with pea jacket worn over the sailor's pullover shirt. There was a popular, though prohibited, fashion in the Navy to shorten the pea jackets as far as possible. This can be seen on the jacket on the right, which has been shortened to be barely longer than waist length. (Heinrich Böhm)**

on field grey for naval land units or gold on tan for tropical kit. A metal pin-on version was also often used on tropical or summer kit. A similar range of national emblems in the same colours was worn on the headdress, at the front of the crown. Beneath the national emblem was a cockade in the national colours for lower ranks; this cockade was surrounded by a wreath of oak leaves on peaked caps worn by warrant and commissioned officers.

Buttons worn on naval clothing displayed a fouled anchor, and were usually gilt finish but painted examples in olive or dark blue were often used on combat or working dress.

Rank insignia was normally embroidered in yellow on dark blue for the blue uniform, yellow on field grey for naval land units or blue on white for summer wear. For junior grades, rank was indicated by a system of chevrons. Trade insignia were worn on the upper left sleeve above the chevron, whilst below the chevron was worn the insignia of a specialist skill held. The specialist insignia was generally embroidered in red, on dark-blue or white backing as appropriate.

For petty officers, a combined rank/trade patch was worn, which consisted of the emblem of their specialist trade superimposed upon a fouled anchor. For chief petty officers, this emblem sat over a single chevron. Special versions of petty officer/chief petty officer insignia were available in gilt metal at the wearer's own expense and were predominantly used on such items as parade jackets.

Warrant officers indicated their rank by shoulder straps, whilst officers indicated their rank by sleeve rings in traditional fashion on the reefer jacket and frock coat, but used shoulder straps on other forms of dress such as the greatcoat, the tropical/summer tunics and the U-boat denim blouse. Confusingly, for a short period in 1943, officers could wear both shoulder straps and sleeve rings on their tunics.

The form of dress adopted by the typical Kriegsmarine seaman was the traditional 'square rig', which consisted of wide-legged trousers and pullover shirt, in dark-blue melton cloth, with the so-called 'Nelson' collar in cornflower blue with three white edge stripes, closely modelled on the British pattern. A sailor's cap was worn, bearing a cap ribbon showing the name of the sailor's vessel or shore establishment. The German style was for the loose ends of the ribbon to hang down from the rear of the cap in 'swallowtail' fashion. The inscription on the cap ribbon was initially woven in gold wire, gothic script on black silk. This was later changed to an easily read yellow cotton thread weave, due to the tendency of the gold wire versions to tarnish to a dull copper colour in salt air, making the lettering difficult to discern. In 1938, a new universal ribbon with the simple legend 'Kriegsmarine' was introduced, and was worn for security reasons, much as the simple 'HMS' ribbon replaced named ship's tally ribbons in the Royal Navy. As the war progressed, the sailor's cap tended to be relegated to parade or formal wear, being replaced for everyday duties by the popular *Bordmutze*, or boarding cap, a side cap made from dark-blue wool.

The basic rig was worn by all ranks up to chief petty officer. It was produced in dark blue for winter wear or in white, with contrasting blue cuffs to the shirt, for summer wear. Tops and trousers from both types were frequently intermixed. Yellow insignia was worn on the dark-blue rig and cornflower-blue insignia on the white rig. The sailor's cap too, was made with both dark blue or white tops.

Naval parade dress, the so-called Affenjacke, or monkey jacket – very smart, but not very functional. In this case the sailors are wearing blue uniform but with white tops to their caps. Colours were often mixed, and the white pullover worn with blue trousers, etc. The Matrosengefreiter at right wears the normal service dress pea jacket. (Jak P. Mallmann Showell)

In cold weather, a dark-blue, heavy wool double-breasted pea jacket was worn over the shirt, with the Nelson collar of the shirt worn inside the jacket. The jacket featured cornflower-blue collar patches with a single row of gilt braid for petty officers and a double row for chief petty officers. The collar of the pea jacket itself was edged with gold braid for PO ranks.

For parade and formal occasions, a short waist-length parade jacket, often referred to as the *Affenjacke*, or monkey jacket, similar in style to a mess jacket, was worn. This had an elaborate double row of gilt naval buttons at the front as well as a row of buttons on each cuff, and was fastened by a gold chain. With this jacket, the Nelson collar was worn outside the jacket.

Warrant officers wore dress much more akin to that worn by commissioned officers, consisting of straight-legged trousers, a white shirt with black tie and a double-breasted reefer jacket. This form of dress was typically worn with a peaked service cap. The cap could have a dark-blue or white top, featured a woven black mohair band, and had a shiny leather peak and chinstrap. After the outbreak of war, the white top was rarely worn by NCO ranks on their peaked caps. A white summer dress was also produced, but in this case the jacket was single breasted with four patch pockets.

Officers wore similar dress to warrant officers, but with the rank indicated by sleeve rings in typical navy fashion. Officer's peaked caps also

ABOVE LEFT **Torpedomechaniker Henrich Böhm, who served on Z17 *Diether von Roeder*, one of the destroyers lost at Narvik, wears both the Destroyer War Badge, and on his left arm above the rank/trade badge, the Narvik Campaign Shield. Böhm transferred to U-boats, serving on U-377, and survived the war. (Heinrich Böhm)**

ABOVE CENTRE **Naval officer caps were superbly executed examples of the hatter's craft. Here, Generaladmiral Saalwachter wears the peaked cap for admiral ranks, with its double row of hand-embroidered gilt-wire oak leaves on the peak. The oak leaf wreath on the band and the national emblem above were also finely hand-embroidered in gilt wire.**

indicated, not specific rank, but rank grouping by the degree of embroidery on the cloth-covered peak of their service cap, or *Schirm-mutze*. For ranks up to Kapitän-leutnant, a narrow row of scalloped gilt embroidery edged the peak. For ranks up to Kapitän zur See, the scalloped design was replaced by a single wide row of oak leaves and for admiral ranks, by a double row of oak leaves. For cold weather wear, officers and warrant officers also had the use of a warm, dark-blue wool double-breasted greatcoat (for admiral ranks this had pale-blue lapel facings).

These were the basic forms of normal service dress. There was, however, a large range of additional specialist clothing worn by KM seamen for specific tasks or duties, many of which will be seen in the photos accompanying this book.

Working dress

Seamen were issued with what could easily be confused at first glance with the white summer rig, but was actually intended as working dress. Rather perversely, in view of some of the filthy tasks which were undertaken wearing this dress, it was cut from white, hard-wearing canvas. No national emblem or contrasting cuffs were worn, which will help identify this dress on photographs. The pullover shirt for this form of dress also featured a single breast pocket. This rig would be worn for all sorts of duties and would end up absolutely filthy, but was hard-wearing and easily washable.

Working jacket

A working jacket in hard-wearing denim was also produced. This was a single-breasted garment with two patch pockets on the shirt. It came in a variety of colours, but most often greenish-brown or olive. From photographic evidence, it seems to have been particularly widely used by PO and CPO ranks.

Leather engine-room clothing

This form of clothing had its origins in the Kaiser's navy. It was produced in various colours, predominantly black or pale grey, but brown versions are also known. The grey version was widely used by U-boat crews and the black version by crews of surface ships. The jacket and trousers were cut from supple leather and had a charcoal-grey blanket lining. The jacket was single-breasted with a narrow stand-up collar and no lapels. No insignia was worn on this dress.

ABOVE RIGHT An Oberleutnant zur See of minesweepers in his formal parade uniform with the antiquated frock coat, rarely worn after the outbreak of war, the brocade dress belt and sword. He wears the Iron Cross Second Class and the Commemorative Medal of October 1938 for the annexation of the Sudetenland. Below this is the War Badge for minesweepers.

This Kapitänleutnant is being given a haircut by one of his crewmen. Note that he wears black leather protective trousers with his regulation blue officer's reefer jacket. (Jak P. Mallmann Showell)

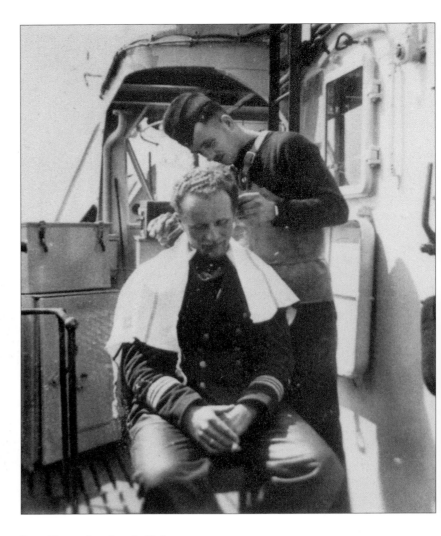

Leather deck clothing

Cut from a similar quality of supple black leather, the deck clothing consisted of leather trousers with an accompanying leather double-breasted three-quarter-length reefer jacket. The wide collar could be turned up to protect the side of the wearer's head in cold weather, when on deck watch, etc.

Tropical kit

A golden tan-coloured single-breasted jacket with open collar, four patch pockets and matching tan trousers was issued for wear in tropical areas and was used by both sea-going personnel and shored-based units, such as naval artillery. Two forms of headgear were used with this rig. The most popular was the peaked field cap, similar to that used by the Afrikakorps, whilst the less popular form was a cumbersome, though light-weight, canvas-covered cork sun helmet. This helmet featured, on its left-hand side, a blackened metal shield with a gilt Wehrmacht style eagle, and on the right, a shield bearing the national colours. These metal insignia mirrored the decals featured on the side of the steel helmet.

Foul-weather gear

All ships carried a supply of foul-weather gear, to include rubberised over-trousers, foul-weather jacket with large collar, and sou'wester hats. None of these were particularly military in appearance and, indeed, given the wide range of suppliers that were contracted, much of it was probably identical to the clothing supplied by these manufacturers to the civilian market – e.g. fishermen, etc.

Sports kit

It was very common in ships operating in warm waters for crewmen to be allowed to wear sports kit comprising shorts and the Navy sports vest – a white singlet with a large, woven, blue-thread national emblem over the chest. This tended to happen less often on large warships where discipline and dress regulations were more rigorously enforced, and more often on smaller vessels such as submarines, S-Boats, minesweepers, etc., where discipline was often far more relaxed.

A junior NCO in the field grey uniform worn by marine artillery personnel. Were it not for the crossed anchors on his shoulder straps and the anchor motif on his buttons, he could, at first glance, pass for an Army soldier, so similar were the uniforms.

Civilian kit

Whilst the use of civilian clothing, such as knitted woollen pullovers, plaid shirts, etc., was common on U-boats, such attire was also often used on the smaller surface ships. It should be pointed out, however, that many such items were also produced and issued as official kit or were captured enemy supplies. In many cases, a mixture of such civilian-style official kit and civilian personal garments provided by the sailors themselves may be seen in photos.

Field grey clothing

The Navy also had its own full range of field grey clothing very similar in its basic form to that worn by the Army. Such field grey clothing could be worn when undergoing basic military training whilst still a recruit, but was also worn by naval coastal artillery units and towards the end of the war by naval infantry units.

The tunic was of single-breasted cut, with closed collar, two exterior patch breast pockets and two interior shirt pockets with only the flap visible. For senior NCO ranks the collar was edged in gold braid. The tunic was worn with field grey trousers and black leather jackboots (replaced by short ankle boots later in the war).

A standard Army-style steel helmet completed the uniform, but in the case of the Navy the eagle decal on the left side was in gilt rather than silver finish. A field grey version of the *Bordmutze* previously described was also produced, as were field grey peaked visor caps for senior NCOs and officers.

This brief overview of the uniforms worn by the typical Kriegsmarine sailor is by no means exhaustive. Many other specialist branches such as the Marineküstenpolizei, naval administrative officials, naval clergy, etc., all had their own distinctive forms of dress. The information here should, however, cover most of the forms of dress that may be seen in the majority of period photographs.

CONDITIONS

Pay

Pay scale for naval personnel was in line with those for the other branches of the armed forces. A number of additions, or *Zulage*, were paid over and above basic pay, for such circumstances as serving in confined spaces (i.e. submarines), serving in the tropics, etc. The standard pay bandings were as follows:

Rank	Payband	Salary (in Reichsmarks)
Matrose	16	1410
Matrosengefreiter	15	1740
Matrosenobergefreiter	15	1740
Matrosenhauptgefreiter	15	1740
Maat	14	2064
Obermaat	13	2322
Feldwebel	12	2394
Oberfeldwebel	11	2454
Stabsfeldwebel	11	2550
Leutnant	10	2400
Oberleutnant	9	3400
Kapitanleutnant	8	4800
Korvettenkapitän	7	7700
Fregattenkapitän	6	9700
Kapitän zur See	5	12600
Konteradmiral	4	16000
Vizeadmiral	3	19000
Admiral	2	24000
Grossadmiral	1	26550

After one year's satisfactory service as a Matrose (Ordinary seaman), a promotion to Matrosengefreiter (able seaman) could be expected, and after a further year at this latter grade, elevation to Matrosenobergefreiter (leading seaman).

For those who had no special ambition for promotion to petty officer, a special grade of Matrosenstabsgefreiter existed for those who had five years satisfactory service as a leading seaman. The rank insignia (two chevrons) was executed in a special plaited braid rather than the normal flat, woven braid to identify these highly experienced but low-ranked seamen.

For servicemen at Matrosenobergefreiter rank, there was no automatic promotion to petty officer, nor was there a facility to apply for promotion. Promotion had to be instigated by the sailor's commanding officer, whose duty it was to identify suitable candidates for promotion

The crew of a minesweeper, seated in the lower ranks' messing area during mealtime. Note the tables are hinged to fold away when not in use. The upright portion of the frame, visible at the left end of each table, is supported by a hook from the ceiling.

to Maat (mate). Once identified, the sailor then had to attend numerous courses to prove his ability to carry out the duties of the higher grade. This included attending the Marineunteroffizierschule, or naval NCO school. Once again, the sailor would almost certainly don field grey uniform and return to exhaustive parade ground and field exercises. This time, however, the training was not intended to test the sailor's abilities as a soldier, but as a potential leader. He would learn to give orders on the parade ground in a firm, authoritative tone, loud and clear with no ambiguity, gaining experience and confidence in himself. Later, he would be tested on the exercise field under simulated combat conditions, so that when giving orders in the heat of battle, he could be depended upon to act in a calm and decisive manner and set a good example to his men. After three years service as a Maat, the sailor might expect to be considered for promotion to Obermaat.

Rations

Servicemen were provided with a regular ration of both ordinary soap and shaving soap, the issue of which was recorded in the pages of their *Soldbuch*. For smokers, a *raucherkarte* (or smoking ration card) was provided to record the issue of a cigarette or tobacco ration.

As well as the normal ration of meals provided by the Wehrmacht, sailors returning on home leave were issued with the so-called *Führer-Packete*, a special issue of rations including chocolate, sweets and other delicacies intended to show those at home how well their fighting men were being treated.

Those destined for service outside of the Reich were issued with small guidance leaflets, or *Merkblätter*, with hints and tips on issues such

as avoiding diseases in areas where malaria was rife, avoiding the risk of cholera, general medical/hygiene advice and instructions on general behaviour. These were printed on small A6 sheets designed to fit neatly inside the serviceman's *Soldbuch*.

Discipline

Though we have seen that the Navy was less politically indoctrinated than some of the other military branches of the Third Reich, and while strings were often pulled to protect sailors who had fallen foul of the authorities in some way, this should not be taken to imply that discipline within the Navy was lax. Those who offended against the Navy's code of honour could expect the severest punishments. This was particularly so towards the end of the war when discipline and morale began to suffer. Those who showed open signs of defeatism or lack of moral fibre, whilst others continued to make sacrifices at the front, were swiftly dealt with.

On one occasion in mid-April 1945, Kriegsmarine shore-based personnel on Heligoland were preparing to surrender to the British. Their signals to the enemy

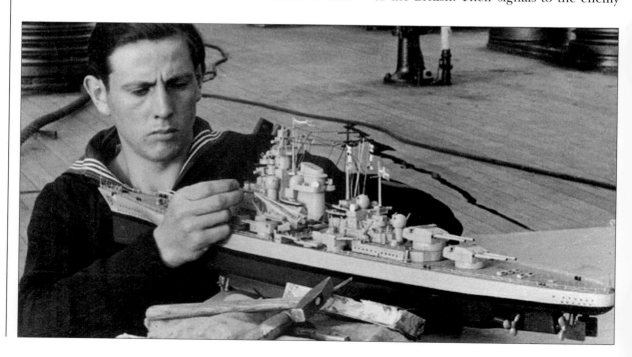

arranging the surrender details were intercepted, however, and a small detachment of S-boats ferried an SS unit out from the mainland to round up and execute the ringleaders, whose corpses were unceremoniously dumped into an unmarked common grave.

A naval *Soldbuch* in the possession of the author contains an entry showing the owner to have been convicted of some unspecified offence by a Field Court Martial on the orders of Reichsführer-SS Heinrich Himmler on 10 April 1945. One week later he was issued with combat equipment and a rifle. One week subsequent to this, he was issued iron rations and sent to the thick of the fighting on the Eastern Front, where within a few days his right leg was blown off in heavy fighting. Fortunately he survived, and having been considered to have redeemed his honour in combat, was awarded the Iron Cross First Class.

The armed forces were also very strict in enforcing discipline amongst their own troops in the occupied territories with looting, theft, assault and other offences being very severely dealt with. Of course, much of this depended on the locals being confident enough to make a

OPPOSITE TOP **All servicemen were issued with *Merkblatter*, or advice leaflets, on myriad subjects. These were to be kept in the inside back cover of the *Soldbuch*. Shown here are tips on how to avoid malaria and dysentery (*Ruhr*), first aid tips, and one with instructions on how to act in the event of air raids, issued by the military command in Vienna. A vast range of such hints and tips were published.**

OPPOSITE BOTTOM **Model-making has always been a popular hobby amongst seamen. This Matrosengefreiter has spent his free time making a highly accurate wooden scale model of his ship, the *Tirpitz*. (Naval Historical Center)**

LEFT **Naval discipline could on occasion be swift and harsh. This photo shows pages from the *Soldbuch* of a Kriegsmarine sailor. The entry at top left indicates that he has been found guilty (crime not specified) at a trial by the Commander of Naval Forces in Pomerania (Seekommandant Pommern) on 10 April 1945 and sentenced to serve with a punishment unit at the front. At top right, his *Soldbuch* shows an entry for the issue of a rifle and bayonet on 19 April, and for 'iron rations' on 24 April. Subsequently thrown into the thick of the fighting on the Eastern Front, the lower entry shows his admittance to the Luftwaffe hospital at Nutschau on 3 May 1945 for amputation of his left leg, a mere 23 days after being sentenced.**

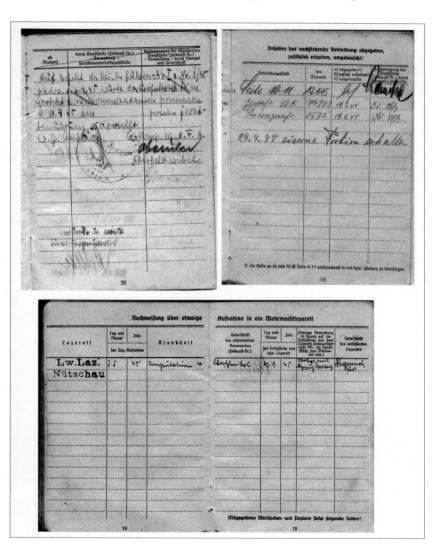

A task beloved of all sailors since time immemorial – swabbing the decks.

complaint to the German authorities in the first place, something that many may not have been prepared to do. However, if complaints were made, they were usually investigated fully and the miscreants often dealt with most harshly.

Apart from general service conditions that affected all Kriegsmarine personnel, there were, of course, others that were more specific to the branch of the Navy in which the individual served.

Generally speaking, conditions were often less favourable in the smaller vessels involved in coastal operations. These would include the minesweepers, the R-boats, S-boats and numerous other smaller auxiliary craft. Whilst many of the larger minesweepers were fairly modern craft, some of the others were former civilian craft, such as trawlers, which had been pressed into military service. Such vessels were usually perfectly seaworthy, but they were often far from comfortable vessels on which to serve. Quarters were usually cramped and facilities poor, but, as these vessels usually operated fairly close inshore and were not often away from their home port for any great length of time, crew comforts were not a matter of much concern.

On the plus side, at least from the crew's point of view, discipline on such smaller vessels was often more relaxed, such ships usually being commanded by relatively junior officers. Many photographs of the crews of such vessels show them wearing forms of dress chosen more for comfort than appearance, much in the same way as with U-boat crews.

On small to medium warships, such as destroyers, with crews of around 325 or so, discipline was a bit more formal, though the relatively small size of the crew meant that close bonds of comradeship would still

Time for relaxation, some cake, and a cup of coffee. The usual formality of larger surface vessels was often relaxed on smaller craft, as evidenced by the chequered shirt and sleeveless pullover worn by the junior officer at the right. (Jak P. Mallmann Showell)

Loading a torpedo into its tube on one of the older Kriegsmarine torpedo boats. These boats were really more like small destroyers, and not at all like the fast motor torpedo boats (MTBs) used by the Allies. The amount of sheer physical effort required for this task can be clearly seen.

Serving on a large battleship was almost like living in a small town. This stern view of the *Bismarck* shows just how huge she was. Note the diminutive size of the crewmen standing on the sternmost turret (turret 'Dora'). (Naval Historical Center)

be formed, with each man knowing most if not all of his crewmates by name. Most of the German destroyers of the Second World War were large, powerful warships (over 3,000 tons fully laden) in comparison with the average Allied destroyer. They were all-new, ultra-modern vessels, but in this lay one of their greatest drawbacks. They featured new, technically advanced steam turbine systems, allowing speeds of well over 35 knots, but which regularly failed. Some destroyers spent almost as much of their wartime career out of action for repairs as they did in service. Most of the German destroyers were sleek, handsome-looking vessels, but like most destroyers in any navy, suffered somewhat in heavy seas, and were rather cramped and uncomfortable vessels on which to serve.

On major warships such as battleships and battlecruisers, the crews were much better provided for. Particularly large battleships such as the *Bismarck* and *Tirpitz*, with crews in excess of 2,000 men, were almost like small cities, boasting their own laundries, bakeries, tailors and cobblers sections, and well-provided mess rooms with upholstered seats, etc.

Of course such huge ships were commanded by officers of senior rank, and often also accommodated a commanding admiral. Naturally then, everything would be expected to be kept spick and span

and sailors would be kept busy scrubbing decks, polishing or painting or any one of a thousand other tasks. The sailors themselves would be expected to be well turned out at all times, and any infringements of dress code could be expected to bring swift retribution with even more hard, manual graft.

On heavy elements of the surface fleet, such battleships and battlecruisers, life tended to be much more regimented and follow a set daily pattern. The following routine would be fairly typical for a seaman serving on a capital ship, such as the *Bismarck* or *Tirpitz*, where the large crew would be split into 12 divisions. Divisions 1 to 6 manned the main, secondary and anti-aircraft armament, division 7 was the support elements such as clerks, cooks, carpenters, etc., division 8 was ordnance, division 9 communications (radio operators and signallers) and divisions 10 to 12 engineering personnel.

0600 Reveille
0630 Breakfast
0715 Fatigues (cleaning, sweeping the decks, etc.)
0800 General maintenance duties (on guns, engines, mechanical equipment, etc.)
1130 Break (Lunch, etc.)
1330 Repeat of morning duties as above
1700 Evening meal
1830 Fatigue duties as in morning
1900 Off duty
2200 Sack time

ABOVE LEFT **Keeping the 2,000-man-plus crew of the *Tirpitz* from becoming bored in their lonely outpost in the far north was a constant challenge for the ship's officers. Here, they have been fortunate enough to secure a visit from an entertainment troupe whose dancers are performing on the quarterdeck under the huge 38 cm guns of turret 'Dora'. (Naval Historical Center)**

ABOVE RIGHT **This photo shows a crew member from one of the auxiliary cruisers. The auxiliary cruiser War Badge is worn on the left breast. In normal service, auxiliary cruiser crewmen were more likely to be disguised as merchant seamen rather than wearing full regulation naval service dress, as shown here. (U-Boot Archiv)**

Those who served on such warships did so with immense pride, with no efforts spared to raise and maintain morale. Sporting competitions between the ship's divisions, concerts by the ship's band, shipboard-produced newspapers, etc., all served to maintain *esprit de corps* and contribute to the sense of satisfaction from serving on such huge and powerful vessels. However, with such huge crews, many men would only get to know their own immediate circle of comrades, so such vessels lacked the close sense of familiarity and confidence between comrades that would be found on small vessels such as U-boats.

One more unusual group of servicemen were those which crewed the auxiliary cruisers. These converted merchant ships would set off alone and unescorted, and roam the seas for months at a time looking for unsuspecting enemy merchantmen to sink. In many cases, crewmen were in fact former merchant seamen who had served on the ships before they had been handed over to the Navy, and were familiar with them and their mechanical idiosyncrasies. Crews of such ships, having to work closely together for months at a time, formed very close bonds of comradeship and, as with the U-boats, strict discipline took second place to trusting each other's skills and abilities. Many auxiliary cruiser captains, such as the chivalrous Bernhard Rogge of the *Atlantis*, took a fatherly interest in the welfare of his men. On one occasion, after issuing bottles of beer to his men to celebrate a victory, he found one of them pouring the beer away. When he asked what was wrong, he was told the crewmen's refrigerator had broken and the beer was warm. Meanwhile, the officers were taking a glass of chilled champagne for their celebratory drink. Rogge immediately ordered that no chilled drinks would be served to officers whilst his men went without. Whilst crewmen were allowed, or in most cases encouraged, not to adopt too smart an appearance lest an eagle-eyed observer with binoculars on an enemy ship spot this and become suspicious (merchant ships not being known for the smartness in appearance of many of their crewmen), Rogge always insisted his officers dress smartly and wear a bow-tie.

Whilst a humane and considerate commander, Rogge would not tolerate dishonesty or dishonourable conduct. When one captive British officer aboard *Atlantis* complained that his binoculars had been stolen, Rogge tracked down the German thief, court-martialled him and sentenced him to three months' imprisonment. So, it can be seen that even where a more relaxed form of discipline was practised, anyone who acted in a dishonourable manner could expect swift punishment. This was not only a matter of honour, as Rogge explained, but a case of setting an example so that the other members of the crew were made well aware of the results of such conduct.

Like military units the world over, the Navy was fond of its mascots. Here we see the 'Scottie' dog adopted as a mascot by the crew of the destroyer *Diether von Roeder*, later sunk at the battle of Narvik. (Heinrich Böhm)

COMBAT ACTION

It would be extremely difficult to give a representative example of combat action for the Kriegsmarine. Active combat service on a small coastal vessel such as an S-boat (E-boat) was as different from combat service on a battleship as it was from combat service in the Coastal Artillery. In this section, therefore, we will look at combat service in the Navy in five basic areas:

Small coastal vessels such as S-boats, R-boats,
    minesweepers, etc.;
Medium sized ocean-going vessels such as
    destroyers and light cruisers;
Large surface ships such as heavy cruisers and
    battleships;
The Kleinkampfmittelverbände; and
Naval land units.

Coastal Operations

A large proportion of the Navy was involved in local coastal operations. These included minesweeping and minelaying, anti-submarine patrols, escort duties (including escorting submarines between port and deeper water), air–sea rescue duties, flak boat and S-boat duties. Many of the vessels involved in these activities were the unsung heroes of the Navy, carrying out essential duties but rarely having the chance to bathe in the kind of glory which the successes of the U-boats or capital ships brought their crews. Minesweeping, however, was a task not without considerable risk.

ABOVE **A minesweeper pulls into its berth. Note the diving eagle emblem painted either side of the bridge. Kriegsmarine minesweepers were relatively large and robust craft which gave excellent service throughout the war.**

LEFT **One of the more unpleasant tasks awaiting junior crew members of some of the older steam driven vessels was coaling. Here, some crew members of a minesweeper are just about to load coal into their ship's bunkers. Note how grubby the white work uniforms became, perhaps the reason that some have elected to wear the black leather engine-room dress. It is assumed this photo was taken just before rather than just after the coaling operation, as the men's faces are too clean to have just completed the task. (Jak P. Mallmann Showell)**

A: THE NEW RECRUIT
(see plate commentary for full details)

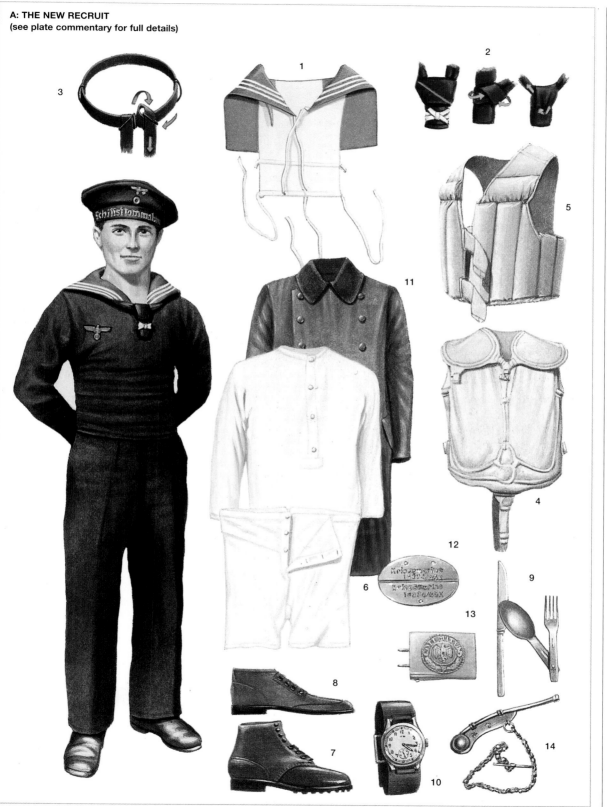

A

B: TRAINING

C: MAINTENANCE
(see plate commentary for full details)

1

2

3

2

4

3

1

A

F: THE AUXILIARY CRUISER
(see plate commentary for full details)

1

3

4

2

F

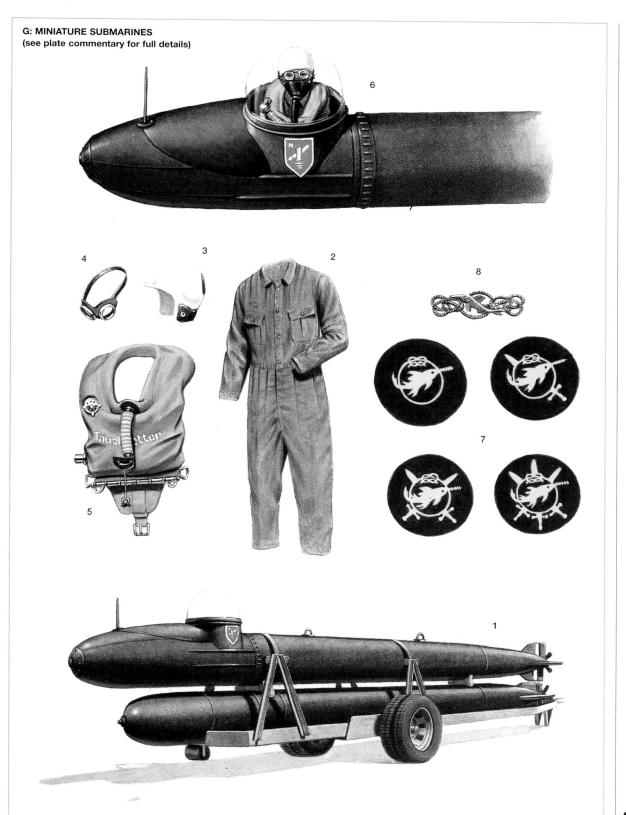

G: MINIATURE SUBMARINES
(see plate commentary for full details)

G

H: LAND-BASED NAVAL SERVICE

There is no shortage of photographic evidence of minesweepers in dry dock for repairs with horrendous damage to the ships' hulls from exploding mines. It is perhaps worthy of note that at least one example of the Minesweeper War Badge was issued with a diamond-studded swastika, a sign that its wearer had been awarded the distinction of the oak leaves to the highly coveted Knight's Cross of the Iron Cross. The Kriegsmarine had a very large fleet of minesweepers, many of which remained in service well after the war, taken over by the GMSA (German Mine Sweeping Administration) and operated under the control of the Royal Navy, clearing thousands of lethal mines from around Europe's coastline. Although there was always a risk of attack by enemy aircraft, especially in the second half of the war, the greatest risk to minesweeper crewmen was from the deadly mines they toiled to clear.

S-boats, of course, made a much more aggressive contribution to Germany's war effort. The German S-boats (*Schnellboot* or fast boat, generally referred to as E-boats by the Allies) were much larger and more powerfully armed than their typical Allied equivalent. Capable of achieving speeds in excess of 40 knots, these 90-ton vessels carried four torpedoes, as well as 2 cm and 4 cm cannons. A total of 32 S-boat flotillas was ultimately raised, each with around 10–12 boats.

The S-boats only began to be fully utilised after the fall of France when the Channel ports fell into German hands. S-boats based in the Channel ports constantly harried Allied shipping and scored many successes, the Channel becoming known as 'S-boat Alley'. Given that the S-boats operating in the west (predominantly in the English Channel and the North Sea) were, throughout the entire war, heavily outnumbered by the Royal Navy, they achieved much, both in tonnage sunk or damaged by the S-boats themselves, or by the mines they laid in

The crew of the minesweeper M3 assembled on the fo'c'sle of their ship, with the commander seated at the centre of the front row. Note the large bronze eagle mounted to the centre of the bridge.

An S-boat at speed in relatively calm seas. These fast and powerful vessels, the 'greyhounds of the sea', gave excellent service in the coastal waters of the North Sea, the Mediterranean, the Baltic, Aegean and Black Seas and were also very efficient minelayers.

British coastal waters. As the war progressed, however, fuel shortages on the German side and growing Allied air power on the other began to curtail operations. Although the S-boats were fast and relatively powerfully armed, they were not designed to take heavy punishment, relying instead on their speed and manoeuvrability to get them out of trouble. When British destroyers using radar intercepted them, they tended to suffer badly.

On the night of 4 September 1940, S-boats of 1 Flotille attacked a small British convoy in the Channel and sank five ships totalling just over 7,000 tons and seriously damaged a 1,300-tonner. By the end of the year over 30 enemy vessels (including at least six warships) totalling in excess of 70,000 tons had been sunk or seriously damaged by S-boats. The following year saw S-boat activity increase and, despite many fiercely contested running battles with British MTBs, well over 30 enemy ships, including the destroyer HMS *Exmoor*, were sunk, totalling over 80,000 tons. Successes were harder to find in 1942, as Allied defences were beefed up. More and more S-boats were damaged or lost in combat with British MTBs, destroyers or aircraft. British use of radar to detect S-boats waiting in ambush was also proving very effective. A total of 28 ships of some 38,000 tons total weight were sunk, though a number of small naval auxiliary vessels such as armed trawlers were also claimed by S-boats. A very lean year followed in 1943, with only 16 enemy ships totalling 26,000 tons being sunk by S-boats.

Prior to the Allied invasion of Normandy in June 1944, a poorly escorted practice landing at Slapton Sands on the south coast of England was intercepted by S-boats and two landing ships sunk and another damaged, with the loss of around 1,000 lives. After the invasion, a number of landing ships and landing craft were sunk by S-boats, as were a small number of MTBs and merchant vessels, but such victories were becoming harder to achieve and only after serious losses to the Germans. For the last year of the war, the most important aspect of the S-boats contribution to the war effort was in mine-laying.

S-boats serving in the Baltic tended to be those on training duties, until the reverses on the Eastern Front brought increasing Soviet naval activity. There were few ship-to-ship engagements between S-boats and

Soviet vessels, the German vessels being used mostly for mine-laying. S-boats were also highly active in the Mediterranean, Aegean and Black Seas, where they gave excellent service both as torpedo boats and as minelayers.

Destroyers and Light Cruisers

The Kriegsmarine began the war with a destroyer force of some 22 vessels. The destroyer fleet was eventually divided into a total of eight flotillas, though it is believed that the 7th Flotilla was never made operational. These were all modern warships, more powerful than their Royal Navy counterparts. The typical main armament of five 5.9-inch guns, as well as two quadruple torpedo tubes, took them nearer to the armament of some light cruisers. On the downside, these sleek, stylish-looking vessels were dogged by poor seaworthiness. They were very 'wet' ships whose fo'c'sles were too short, causing them to ship huge amounts of water in rough seas, so much so that the forward gun turret would often be unusable. They also suffered from somewhat limited range and severe technical problems with their advanced propulsion systems, being driven by superheated steam turbines, which gave a possible top speed in excess of 38 knots. Many of these vessels seemed to spend more time out of service with breakdowns than they did ready for action.

As the war progressed, attempts were made to improve destroyer design. Eventually, 56 vessels were constructed, the latter examples featuring a large twin 5.9-inch turret forward, whose massive weight did nothing to help the ship's seaworthiness. German destroyers, in anything much more than a moderately heavy sea, were not pleasant vessels on which to serve. Constant pitching and tossing in heavy seas did little to help accuracy with either gunfire or torpedoes.

Snapshot of the destroyer *Diether von Roeder,* taken by one of its former crewmen. Fast and powerful, these destroyers had advanced propulsion systems which were dogged by technical problems. This vessel was one of many sunk during the battle of Narvik. The pennant number on her hull side was not the ship's own number (*Diether von Roeder* was *Z17*) but the flotilla number and the ship's number within the flotilla – 51= 5th ship, 1st flotilla. (Heinrich Böhm)

In the early part of the war, however, the destroyer force did excellent service in a mine-laying capacity. The first major engagement with enemy surface warships proved disastrous. More than half the total destroyer strength, some 12 vessels, were caught unawares and sunk by a British task force including the battleship HMS *Warspite* in Narvik Fjord during the invasion of Norway. Subsequently, destroyers were used principally on escort duties: accompanying convoys, U-boats between their bases and deep water and capital ships moving to and from bases in Norway.

Four destroyers also took part in the successful 'Channel dash', escorting the battlecruisers *Scharnhorst* and *Gneisenau* and the heavy cruiser *Prinz Eugen* through the English Channel under the very noses of the Royal Navy. An attempted strike on Allied convoys in December 1942, Operation 'Regenbogen' (Rainbow), saw the heavy cruisers *Hipper* and *Lützow*, escorted by a number of destroyers, run into the British heavy cruisers *Sheffield* and *Jamaica*. The subsequent action was a disaster for the Germans, with *Hipper* badly damaged and the destroyer *Friedrich Eckoldt*, mistaking *Jamaica* for *Hipper*, approaching too close and being battered at point-blank range by the British ship's heavy guns. The German destroyer was lost with all hands.

Destroyers accompanied the battlecruiser *Scharnhorst*'s last action. Her escort of five destroyers, however, was despatched to hunt down the British convoy, leaving *Scharnhorst* without a protective screen. She was attacked and sunk by the battleship *Duke of York* and the heavy cruiser *Belfast*.

Destroyers spent the final part of the war in support operations in the Baltic, and saved many civilian refugees from the advancing Red Army.

There were six light cruisers serving with the Kriegsmarine at the outbreak of war: *Emden*, *Köln*, *Königsberg*, *Karlsruhe*, *Leipzig* and *Nurnberg*. These light cruisers contributed little to the war. *Karlsruhe* and *Königsberg* were lost during the invasion of Norway, the first being mortally damaged by a torpedo hit from a British submarine, requiring her to be finished off by a German torpedo boat, and the second, like *Blücher*, lost to gunfire from a shore battery. *Leipzig* was also badly damaged by an enemy torpedo and was relegated to training duties. Recalled to fleet service in 1944, she was accidentally rammed by *Prinz Eugen*, an incident which finished her service career. *Köln*, *Nurnberg* and *Emden* were predominantly used as training vessels in the Baltic.

Major Warships (Battleships and Cruisers)

The German fleet began the war with only a small number of capital ships compared to the Allies. These, however, were all modern vessels, fast and with powerful armament. There were two major battleships, the *Bismarck* and *Tirpitz*, two heavy battlecruisers, *Scharnhorst* and *Gneisenau*, three so-called Panzerschiffe, or pocket battleships (later redesignated as heavy cruisers), the *Admiral Graf Spee*, *Deutschland* and *Admiral Scheer*, three heavy cruisers, the *Admiral Hipper*, the *Blücher* and the *Prinz Eugen*. In addition, the old pre-dreadnoughts, *Schlesien* and *Schleswig-Holstein*, though not fit for major surface action against enemy ships, gave good service both as training ships and in shore bombardment in the Baltic. The German capital ships were never intended for action against other battleships, however, but for raiding on the merchant vessels which provided Britain's lifeline in times of war.

The large ships such as *Bismarck* and *Tirpitz* mounted superb, high-quality 15-inch main armament. These massive ships provided a very stable gun platform for their main armament and were so well designed and constructed that former crew members relate that, even on firing a broadside from her main armament, there was little tendency to sideways movement or to heel over with the recoil of the big guns. This allowed for very accurate shooting. They maintained great stability even in a moderately heavy swell and evinced little engine vibration even at high speeds. The crews of these ships were extremely proud and confident of their vessels. The story of the *Bismarck* is too well known to

A highly atmospheric shot of the mighty battleship *Tirpitz* in Ka Fjord, Norway. On a dark, overcast day, the ship itself has been illuminated by a ray of sunshine, highlighting it against the grim landscape and forbidding sky. (Naval Historical Center)

ABOVE LEFT **The imposing bulk of the *Tirpitz* can be clearly seen as she is manoeuvred into position at her mooring in Ka Fjord by a naval tug. (Naval Historical Center)**

ABOVE RIGHT **The beautiful but desolate scenery of *Tirpitz*'s lair can be seen in this photo, as a group of crewmen assemble under the guns of turret 'Bruno'. Of interest is the small group of men in lighter uniforms at bottom right. These are Luftwaffe airmen who crewed the ship's Arado 196 seaplanes. Also of note is the vaulting-horse which sits at bottom left ready for PT on deck. (Naval Historical Center)**

warrant repeating here, but the ship was certainly a match for any other battleship in the world on equal terms. She was brought to battle by an overwhelmingly superior British force, after sinking the pride of the Royal Navy, HMS *Hood*, and was herself sunk in 1941.

Subsequently, her sister ship, *Tirpitz*, was to spend the rest of her life hidden away in a Norwegian fjord, where she was finally sunk by RAF bombers in 1944. Despite her inactivity, the mere threat that *Tirpitz* might emerge from hiding for an attack on Allied shipping was a constant nightmare for the British, and tied down many resources until her eventual sinking.

Scharnhorst and her sister, *Gneisenau*, did achieve modest success as surface raiders in the Atlantic and achieved a propaganda coup for Germany in the successful 'Channel Dash'. *Gneisenau* was badly damaged by Allied bombing raids in February 1942, which paid dividends on 1 July that year; she was sunk by the Germans as a blockship in Gotenhafen harbour, a rather ignominious end for this beautiful ship. *Scharnhorst* was finally sunk after a brief but furious battle with the battleship *Duke of York* and the heavy cruiser *Belfast* after an attempt to intercept an Allied convoy off the North Cape in December 1943. Only 36 of her crew of 1,968 were saved.

These ships, the size of battleships, and indeed classed as battleships by the Kriegsmarine, had only 11-inch guns and should therefore only be considered as battlecruisers. It was intended to replace their 11-inch triple turrets with 15-inch twin turrets of the type used in *Bismarck*, but this was never achieved. They were extremely 'wet' ships that were much less stable than *Bismarck* or *Tirpitz* in heavy seas. Nevertheless, they were known as 'Happy Ships' and were much loved by their crews.

Graf Spee, after a fairly successful cruise as a commerce raider, was brought to battle by a British cruiser squadron in the South Atlantic. *Graf Spee* wreaked havoc on her attackers but suffered damage herself. Taking refuge in neutral Montevideo harbour, her captain was fooled into thinking that a much larger force lay in wait for him than was actually the case, and scuttled his ship to prevent her being defeated in battle or captured by the enemy.

Deutschland (renamed *Lützow*) took part in the ill-fated battle of the Barents Sea when she, in collaboration with *Admiral Hipper* and a number of destroyers, attempted to attack the Russian convoy routes. Confronted by two Royal Navy cruisers and several destroyers, the *Hipper* was badly damaged when a 6-inch shell penetrated below her waterline. (The Germans had a firepower advantage over the British, *Hipper* mounting 8-inch guns and *Lützow* 11-inch guns against the 6-inch guns mounted by both British cruisers.) The Germans broke off and retreated to their base. Hitler was enraged at the lack of aggressiveness shown by his captains and threatened to scrap the entire surface fleet. *Lützow* spent the latter part of the war in the Baltic with *Prinz Eugen* on fire support duties for the Army.

Like her near sister, *Admiral Graf Spee*, the *Admiral Scheer* scored some moderate successes as a surface raider on her first major war cruise between October 1940 and March 1941, sinking 14 merchant ships and one British auxiliary cruiser. Thereafter, she spent an uneventful spell in the Baltic before transferring to Norway. She never again enjoyed the level of success of her war cruise in the early part of the war, and probably her greatest achievement in the closing stages of the war was the successful evacuation of over 1,000 refugees and wounded from Pillau. She was hit in a RAF bombing raid and capsized in harbour at Kiel on 9–10 April 1945.

The 10.5 cm shells for the twin anti-aircraft mounts on *Bismarck/Tirpitz* class ships were stored below decks and brought up to the guns in special cradles via elevator shafts. This saved a huge amount of hard, physical effort for the crewmen. These modern battleships had many novel features that made life aboard much easier for the crews. (Naval Historical Center)

A number of crewmen are busy camouflaging their ship against detection by Allied aircraft in this interesting shot of the *Tirpitz* in its Norwegian lair. (Naval Historical Center)

Blücher was destroyed during the invasion of Norway, when she was taken under fire by the guns of the Norwegian shore battery at Dröbak, near Olso. She sank taking a large number of her crew with her on 7 May 1940.

Admiral Hipper was one of the few German cruisers that actually took part in raiding activities. Her first cruise in 1940 was rather uneventful, with only one enemy vessel of some 6,000 tons being sunk; but on her second outing in early 1941, she intercepted Convoy SLS64 and sank seven ships totalling nearly 33,000 tons. After this success she, too, moved to Norway and took part in mine-laying activities off the North Cape. She was also involved in the battle of the Barents Sea in December 1942, where she and *Lützow* were engaged by British cruisers, and *Hipper* suffered heavy damage, requiring her to put into dry dock for repairs. Here she was paid off in February 1943 and languished, unrepaired, until the war's end.

Prinz Eugen, after successfully escaping *Bismarck*'s fate, put in at Brest. From here, she escaped back to Germany during the 'Channel dash' in 1942, in company with *Scharnhorst* and *Gneisenau*. From Germany, she was moved to Norway, and was torpedoed by a British submarine off the Norwegian coast. She was then moved to the Baltic, where she gave fire support to aid the beleaguered German armies on the Eastern Front. She spent several months in the second half of 1944 having her gun barrels relined after shooting off several thousand rounds of ammunition from her main armament. The *Hipper* class heavy cruisers, though fast and well armed, suffered from mechanical problems and had only very limited endurance so that they needed constant attention from oilers when on active service.

The Kleinkampfmittelverbände (K-Verbände).

These small, special-purpose naval units, known as the *K-Verbände*, were established under Konteradmiral (later Vizeadmiral) Helmut Heye in April 1944, and were the nearest thing the German Navy had to a commando/SBS type force. Mention of these units generally brings to mind the one-man torpedo or midget submarine units, and indeed these formed a major part of the K-V, but there were other equally fascinating aspects to this force.

As far as the mini-subs are concerned, several types were planned and built, but in the event, none achieved any significant combat success. The *Neger* was a very simple device consisting of an electrically powered, manned torpedo, in which the operator sat with a flimsy plexiglass dome for protection against the sea. Below this propulsion unit was slung a live G7e torpedo. When placed into the water, the unit became invisible but for the small plexiglass dome. The unit had no capacity to submerge fully. This was a very basic, and very dangerous, piece of equipment, which was liable to become swamped, difficult to control in anything more than a moderate swell, and easily spotted by vigilant lookouts on enemy vessels. They were, however, used operationally, the first combat use being at Anzio against the Allied invasion fleet. Losses, however, were high, with only 13 returning from a total of 23 launched, and the results did not really justify their use, as not a single Allied ship was damaged.

A naval diver in full diving kit prepares to inspect the hull of his ship for damage. The shot seems to have been taken in port. Note the hook attached to the top of his helmet, no doubt designed to suspend him at a fixed depth when carrying out his inspection. Normally, weights carried by the diver would take him to the seabed.

An improved version, the *Marder*, was given a limited dive capability and used against the Allied invasion fleet at Normandy on 5 July 1944. A total of 26 *Marder* were launched, of which 15 were destroyed, for a loss rate of over 50 per cent. This time, however, two British minesweepers were sunk. Three nights later, a further attack by 21 *Marder* succeeded in sinking a further minesweeper and permanently disabling a light cruiser. Subsequent attacks sunk the British destroyer *Quorn*, as well as a small number of landing craft, transports and other auxiliary vessels. Although some successes had been achieved, they were at the cost of considerable losses. Many considered their use almost suicidal, and problems in obtaining enough volunteers began to be experienced. One *Neger* operator, however, Schreibermaat Walter Gerhold, was decorated with the Knight's Cross of the Iron Cross and survived the war.

More advanced designs such as the *Biber*, a miniature submarine carrying two external torpedoes, had even less success. In one operation in December 1944, 18 *Biber* set off from their base

A rather interesting shot showing a number of naval personnel on a motorcycle combination in Norway in 1940. On close examination, a small fouled anchor motif can just be made out on the lapels of the officer driving the motorcycle. He is almost certainly a naval war correspondent covering the aftermath of the battle of Narvik with two of his assistants.

in Holland. One small ship of just less than 5,000 tons was sunk, but every *Biber* was lost. The *Biber* had a disastrous record of losses. One senior naval officer caustically commented that no opinion on their successes could be calculated, as none had ever returned from an operation. From one recovered vessel, it was discovered that petrol fumes from its engine had suffocated the crewman. Many others of those who never returned may have suffered a similar fate. The *Seehunde*, was a slightly more technically advanced mini-submarine, and slightly less dangerous to its operator. One even survived an attack by a British torpedo boat. Nevertheless, rewards for its efforts were scant, with only four enemy ships being sunk in well over 30 sorties by the *Seehunde* type of mini-submarine.

Some idea of the ineffectiveness of these weapons can be gleaned from the fact that in March 1945, from a total of 56 sorties by *Biber* and the newer *Molch* types, over 40 vessels were lost for the sinking of just 250 tons of enemy shipping.

In addition to the mini-submarines, the K-V also used *Linsen*, small, fast motor torpedo boats which were packed full of high explosive and propelled at top speed towards their target. Several *Linsen* and one control boat would be used. The *Linsen* operator would dive overboard at the last possible moment, leaving the boat to be steered to its target by radio from the control boat, the explosives packed into its hull detonating when it hit its target. The *Linsen* crewmen would then be picked up by the control boat. These motor boats were to be used against ships and targets such as bridges, etc. These boats were used operationally but did not achieve many successes, a large number of the boats being lost to mechanical problems or to heavy seas long before the target areas were reached. Like the *Neger* operators, personnel using these boats stood a very high chance of being killed or seriously wounded.

Despite the very low success rate achieved by the Kleinkampf-mittelverbände, there can be no doubting the bravery of the K-men themselves, working in tiny, cramped, primitive vessels, in freezing cold, with choking fumes and with very little prospect of survival. A special insignia, consisting of a sawfish superimposed over a knotted rope, was introduced as a decoration for the men of the Kleinkampfmittelverbände. The extreme rarity of original examples is testimony to how difficult it was to earn, and perhaps also of how few survived.

Naval Land Units

The greatest number of naval land-based troops served in the Marine Artillerie. These troops provided coastal defences in Germany and throughout the occupied territories. Such personnel wore field grey uniforms closely resembling those of the Army but with gilt naval-type insignia. For the greater part of the war, their main task was to contribute to coastal anti-aircraft defences. This being the case, they tended only to see the enemy from a considerable distance, and the greatest danger to them would be from bombs dropped by enemy aircraft. As coastal defences tended to be in heavy, reinforced concrete bunkers, this, until the invasion of the European mainland in 1944, would have been considered a fairly safe posting.

As well as the naval coastal artillery, other auxiliary branches such as naval transport units also served in field grey uniforms. Although initially a relatively safe duty, as Allied air power increased and eventually gave them almost total control of the skies, driving motor transport anywhere in daylight had to be considered a highly risky business. This was especially true in occupied areas, where partisans also had to be contended with.

Finally, towards the end of the war, with many of the fleet's major surface vessels sunk or disabled and even the U-boats struggling to survive, the Kriegsmarine found itself with a glut of manpower. Many of these men were formed into naval infantry units (Marine Infanterie Divisionen) and put into frontline combat service. Here, many trained

Naval artillerymen parade for inspection by their commanding admiral. Once again, note the similarity to uniforms of the Army. Their own commanding officer, standing behind the admiral, also wears field grey.

expert technicians from the fleet and the U-Boot Waffe were lost in infantry actions which could do little if anything to alter the course of events of the war. Nevertheless, all Kriegsmarine personnel had gone through an initial basic training which included infantry skills, and with only brief refresher training of a few days, these sailors gave a good account of themselves on numerous occasions as we have already seen with Korvettenkapitän Cremer's tank-hunting teams.

BELIEF AND BELONGING

A particularly significant factor in understanding the high morale, sense of honour and devotion to duty in the German Navy, is that it was by far the least politically involved of all of the branches of the German military and paramilitary forces. Hitler was a poor sailor, who is said to have once been seasick simply visiting a ship tied up in port. Whilst he was interested in the propaganda value any victories by his Navy would bring him, he had no real interest in ships or in the Navy and its traditions.

Naval regulations were quite strict in that membership of a political party was prohibited. There are many examples of well-known and highly decorated Kriegsmarine sailors who had to give up membership of the Party before taking up their commissions with the Navy. This of course does not mean that there were no Nazis in the Kriegsmarine, one source estimating that over 40 per cent of new officer recruits were former party members. However, it certainly seems that once in the Navy, it was the code of ethics of the Kriegsmarine, not of the Party, that was adhered to. The Navy was very much a conservative, not to say right-wing, organisation, but could never be considered 'Nazi'.

By 1918, the situation on the German home front was becoming more and more unstable. The German left wing, inspired by the revolution in Russia, began to foment unrest. 'Soldier's Councils' were set up and officers were deliberately humiliated, disgraced and, in some extreme cases, executed by their erstwhile subordinates. The Navy, too, had its 'Sailor's Councils' though many naval units, in particular the U-boats, remained fiercely loyal. The disgrace and humiliation felt by many because of this communist-led revolt, and the active part played by many naval volunteer units, or *Freikorps*, in suppressing communism, are evidence of its conservative political stance. However, many former Kriegsmarine personnel have gone on record to say that they honestly believed that the Navy shielded them from National Socialist ideology.

Where Nazi ideals were foisted upon the Navy, they tended to be paid lip service, but were rarely treated with any serious interest.

Well-designed insignia and badges played a large part in boosting general morale and a sense of kinship within branches of the armed forces. Naval war badges were particularly attractive and well executed. Shown here are (top left to bottom right) War Badge for S-boats (first pattern), War Badge for Auxiliary Cruisers, War Badge for Blockade Breakers and War Badge for Major Warships, (known as the Fleet War Badge).

As well as in its own magazine *Die Kriegsmarine* (left), naval exploits were well covered in the illustrated journals of the day, especially those from publishers based in the large seaports, such as the *Hamburger Illustrierte* shown at right.

In some cases, such as when the Nazi-style salute was introduced throughout the armed forces following the abortive attempt to assassinate Hitler in July 1944, the rules tended to be obeyed on formal or public occasions, but ignored when it was felt safe to do so. Certainly, there seems to have been no shortage of occasions when naval personnel clashed with the political authorities, with U-boat men being the worst offenders.

Throughout the entire war, the Kriegsmarine adhered to its own moral codes and sense of honour. It must be reasonable to suggest that there is some link between the fact that the Navy is generally considered as being the least political of the German armed forces, and the fact that the war at sea was far more cleanly fought than the war on land. Again, there is no shortage of incidents of Kriegsmarine personnel acting with great chivalry towards wounded or captured enemy, and there seems to have been considerable mutual respect between the sailors of both sides.

Although the German Navy was a fairly young organisation, it had a fiercely proud tradition. Of course, there were still many rather antiquated vessels in the Kriegsmarine. In fact, the first shots of World War II were fired from the old pre-dreadnought *Schleswig-Holstein*, a relic of the Kaiser's days, which opened fire on the Polish fortress at Westerplatte on 1 September 1939, and her sister ship, the *Schlesien,* was still in action against the Soviets in the battle for Gotenhafen in April 1945. The loss of the High Seas Fleet, scuttled at Scapa Flow in 1919, forced Germany to build anew, so that many of her ships were fast, powerful and ultra-modern. The typical German sailor serving on one

Great pride was taken by seamen in the historical links engendered by the names of their ships. Here, Torpedoman Heinrich Bohm is shown whilst serving pre-war on the pocket battleship *Graf Spee*. His cap ribbon reads 'Panzerschiff Admiral Graf Spee'. Also of interest is the mixing of uniform parts. Previous photos have shown the use of the parade jacket with the blue shirt. Here it is worn with the white shirt, and once again, the white top to the sailor's cap. (Heinrich Böhm)

of these modern vessels was immensely proud of his ship, and every effort was made to encourage unit pride. Ship's crews from the great battleships which bore the names of famous historical individuals such as *Bismarck*, *Tirpitz*, *Scharnhorst* and *Gneisenau*, found that a great deal of tradition was inherited along with the ship's name. Often, descendants of these historic individuals were invited to the official launching ceremony to foster these bonds.

The crews of such ships as the light cruisers that were named after major cities usually formed close relationships with the city for which they were named, and the actions involving these ships were keenly followed by the local press. Even smaller ships such as destroyers were named for heroes of the Great War, including those such as *Bruno Heinemann* and *Wolfgang Zenker* who were killed resisting the so-called sailors' revolution of November 1918. The naming of ships was a matter of no small importance to naval pride. Many of the names used were those of well-known heroes within Germany, little-known, then or now, outside the Fatherland. Thus the men of the Kriegsmarine, though serving in a fairly young branch of the services, had no shortage of the traditional links that are so important to any fighting force. A selection of these are explained in the glossary.

Although the naming of smaller vessels ceased with the onset of war (only the first 22 of the Kriegsmarine's destroyers were named, the others all being simply numbered), every effort was made to instil *esprit de corps* at flotilla level with the introduction of unofficial cap insignia (particularly widespread in the U-boat service) or small honour pins (the so-called *Ehrennadel* which was typically in the form of a small enamelled lapel pin), which were usually accompanied by an elaborate award document.

The uniform worn by a serviceman also played an important part in maintaining morale and instilling pride. There can be no doubt that the service dress worn by the typical German sailor during the life of the Kriegsmarine was particularly elegant. It drew on the best elements of the Royal Navy uniform, and then added its own uniquely German touches to produce an eminently suitable form of naval dress.

One of the most important factors in maintaining morale and a sense of belonging was certainly the award of the appropriate 'war badge' to an active-service sailor. A plethora of badges and insignia was produced during the period of the Third Reich, where even the most humble of jobs seemed to have its own special range of uniforms and insignia. The difference, however, between impressive badges such as the Pilot's Badge of the Luftwaffe and the Fleet War Badge of the Navy was that the former was simply a qualification badge, but the latter had to be earned through wartime combat service.

Top designers, such as Wilhelm Ernst Peekhaus of Berlin, were commissioned to create a range of awards to recognise the participation of sailors in a set number of war cruises. Separate badges were created for the crews of U-boats, destroyers, minesweepers, capital chips, S-boats, auxiliary cruisers, blockade breakers, and coastal flak units. Early examples of such badges were made in the best-quality materials, and finely fire-gilded to give a most attractive appearance. Even later in the war, although the use of cheaper materials was necessary, the quality of the strikings themselves remained high. In some cases, special versions of the badges were manufactured in real silver, gilded and with the swastika held by the eagle national emblem studded with diamonds. These beautiful awards were bestowed, as personal gifts by the Commander in Chief Navy, upon a number of sailors who had been decorated with the oak leaves to the Knight's Cross of the Iron Cross.

The cap band worn by a sailor was in some ways analogous to the cuff titles worn by elite units of the German Army and Airforce. Enormous pride was taken in wearing a band with the name of a famous, powerful ship. Shown here is an original Matrosenmütze with its wartime original example of the 'Schlachtschiff Scharnhorst' ribbon (now, sadly, widely reproduced).

The German fashion was for the full size original version of most military decorations to be worn at all times, even in combat, so a decorated soldier could be easily spotted, and a combat veteran would wear his war badge with great pride. As well as providing the individual with a visible reward for his active service, the war badge would also help maintain morale amongst other, less experienced sailors who could take comfort from the presence of easily identifiable, seasoned combat veterans in their midst.

Many vessels and shore establishments created their own local newssheets or newspapers with unit news, reports on unit members who had been decorated or specially commended, etc. All of this helped to build and maintain morale and a sense of kinship, and most of all a deep sense of pride in having served with the Kriegsmarine. To this day, there are a number of highly active veterans' associations for former crew members of various ships and flotillas, indicating that despite the difficulties in being seen to commemorate anything connected with that period in Germany today, the bonds of comradeship formed during service with the Kriegsmarine are as strong as ever.

COLLECTING

The amount of original Kriegsmarine memorabilia still available to the collector is vast. A huge range of trade and rank patches existed, most of which are still obtainable at very low prices. Even uniforms are relatively inexpensive compared with those of the Army or Luftwaffe. The prices are reflective of the low demand for such items, which tend to be sought by specialist naval collectors, with few general collections of German militaria containing such pieces.

Probably the most popular naval item amongst collectors is the War Badge. In simplistic terms these can be divided into two types, those high-quality pieces made until around 1941–42 and those made in the second half of the war using poorer quality metals.

S-boat ace, Korvettenkapitän Hermann Büchting, winner of the Knight's Cross of the Iron Cross. The S-boat War Badge can be just seen below and to the right of his Iron Cross. Hermann Büchting survived the war and was a regular correspondent with many history enthusiasts, including the author, until he passed away in 1996. (Hermann Büchting)

Early pieces were struck from a bronze alloy, known as Tombak, that was then given a fine fire-gilded finish. The premier manufacturer of naval badges was the firm of Schwerin in Berlin, and early examples with this maker mark fetch a premium price. Regrettably, they are also widely faked and can provide many pitfalls for the unwary. Later badges were die-struck or cast from zinc and given a gold-washed or anodised finish that rarely survived long and ultimately left the badge in an unattractive dull grey colour. Though less attractive to look at, such examples have a greater likelihood of being true wartime originals. Badges were struck for the crews of individual types of vessel. Prices at the time of writing can range from £50 for a minesweeper badge to over £800 for a particularly nice example of the rare 1st type S-boat Badge.

The award documents which accompanied these badges are also highly collectable and in some cases are worth much more than the award itself. Regrettably, like all rare and sought after German items, these, too, are being widely reproduced.

Headgear is also very popular amongst Kriegsmarine collectors. Two types of headgear feature prominently amongst the most popular buys on the memorabilia market, these being the sailor's cap with ship's ribbon, and the peaked cap worn by officers. Numerous photos in this book show both types being worn. Both are now rare in the original. These caps are not often faked as such, but there is a flourishing trade in converted post-war West German Navy caps that, in basic style and construction, are almost identical to their wartime forebears. Prospective buyers should beware of linings made from nylon rather than the original satin or silk, and caps that are assembled using nylon threads. The peaks of Kriegsmarine visor caps are always bound in leather or leatherette fabric, whilst those of the West German Bundesmarine are bound with PVC-type plastic. Most wartime caps were lined in pale to mid-blue satin and have sweat diamonds of cellulose that by now will have gone brittle with age. Caps with white lining, coupled with soft, pliable plastic sweat diamonds should be treated with caution as most post-war caps are of this form.

The removable top of the sailor's cap was lined in black cotton, usually marked with the official clothing stores stamps for Kiel or Wilhelmshaven in white ink. Once again, the modern equivalents make wide use of plastics and nylon threads which will melt if exposed to heat. Cotton threads used at the time will burn to a fine ash.

It should also be borne in mind that in the early days of the West German Navy, cap ribbons in identical styling to those of the Kriegsmarine were used, woven in gold wire or cotton thread Gothic letters on a black silk band. There is no easy way to tell these apart from wartime issues other than familiarising oneself with the ship or shore establishment names to determine which are from the post-war era. Ribbons themselves are rarely faked, though some fantasy bands such as those for *Bismarck*, *Tirpitz* and the aircraft carrier *Graf Zeppelin* have all been made up since the war. There is no record of any originals of these bands ever being made, the biggest warships to have received their own tally ribbons being *Scharnhorst* and *Gneisenau*. So, it can be seen that collecting Kriegsmarine memorabilia can be fraught with danger for the unwary. The best advice that can be given is to buy only from reputable sources which offer a unlimited-time money back guarantee.

MUSEUMS AND ARCHIVES

Although there are very few museums with specialist collections of Kriegsmarine items, many mainstream museums do have a selection of such items on display. The Imperial War Museum in London possesses many fine German Navy exhibits, as well as a sizeable photo archive, and also features a surviving example of the *Biber* type mini-submarine. Nearby, on the Thames, the cruiser *Belfast* is now a floating museum and contains a fine display of exhibits relating to the battle of the North Cape in which the *Scharnhorst* was sunk. The Museum of the Shropshire Light Infantry in Shrewsbury has in its possession the original grand admiral's baton of Grossadmiral Dönitz, that was stolen from Dönitz when he was taken into custody in 1945.

In Germany, the Deutsches Museum in Munich has some extremely rare naval exhibits including a 'cut-away' *Seehund* , a *Biber* , one of the all-electric *Molch* and a *Neger* one-man torpedo, all extremely rare. The German Naval Memorial at Laboe, near Kiel, is also worth visiting for its excellent collection of model warships as well as many rare and original naval banners and flags. The U-boat Archive at Cuxhaven, though predominantly concerned with U-boat history, has a fine collection of

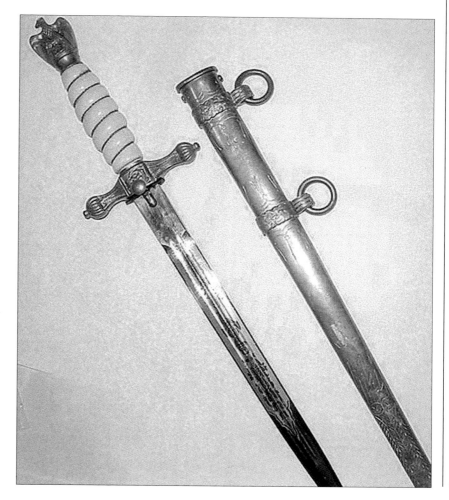

Well aware of the positive effect of well-designed uniforms and accoutrements in boosting morale and the sense of self-esteem of the serviceman, the Germans made great use of edged weapons in the huge range of military regalia they produced. The armed forces were well served by the edged weapons manufacturers, and the naval dagger was one of the most attractive of these. Worn by senior NCOs and officers, it was produced in a variety of qualities including those with hand-made Damascus-steel blades, and even an honour dagger variant with a diamond-studded pommel.

original Kriegsmarine uniforms and insignia on display, which are of interest to all naval collectors. The German Naval Academy at Mürwick also has its own collection (Marineschule Mürwick Historische Sammlung) which includes rare original awards and decorations (including the diamond-studded U-boat badge of submariner Otto Kretschmer) as well as a large photographic archive.

BIBLIOGRAPHY

The following books have been selected because they are very heavily illustrated, with photographs similar to those included in this book, and will give the reader an insight into life in the Kriegsmarine.

Angolia, John R., Schlicht, Adolf, *Kriegsmarine, Uniforms & Traditions, Vol 1*, Bender Publishing, San Jose, 1991

Angolia, John R., Schlicht, Adolf, *Kriegsmarine, Uniforms and Traditions, Vol 2*, Bender Publishing, San Jose, 1991

Angolia, John R., Schlicht, Adolf, *Kriegsmarine, Uniforms and Traditions, Vol 3*, Bender Publishing, San Jose, 1993

Becker, Cajus, *The German Navy 1939–45*, Chancellor Press, London, 1997

Breyer, Siegfried, Koop, Gerhard, *The German Navy at War, Vol 1*, Schiffer Publishing, Pennsylvania, 1989

Breyer, Siegfried, Koop, Gerhard, *The German Navy at War, Vol 2*, Schiffer Publishing, Pennsylvania, 1989

Chazette, Alain, Reberac, Fabien, *Kriegsmarine*, Editions Heimdal, Bayeux, 1997

Elfrath, Ulrich, Herzog, Bodo, *Battleship Bismarck*, Schiffer Publishing, Pennsylvania, 1989

Koop, Gerhard, Schmolke, Klaus-Peter, *Battleships of the Scharnhorst Class*, Greenhill Books, London, 1999

Koop, Gerhard, Schmolke, Klaus-Peter, *Pocket Battleships of the Deutschland Class*, Greenhill Books, London, 2000

Mallmann-Showell, Jak P., *The German Navy in World War Two*, Arms & Armour Press, London, 1979

Mallmann-Showell, Jak P., *German Navy Handbook 1939–45*, Sutton Publishing, Stroud, 1999

Stern, Robert C., *Kriegsmarine: A Pictorial History of the German Navy 1935–45*, Arms & Armour Press, London, 1979

Whitley, M .J., *German Cruisers of World War Two*, Arms & Armour Press, London, 1985

Whitley, M. J., *German Coastal Forces of World War Two*, Arms & Armour Press, London, 1992

In addition to these highly illustrated books, the following predominantly textual titles that give a superb insight into service in the U-Boot Waffe, but are also highly relevant to service in the Germany Navy in general, are also highly recommended.

Mulligan, Timothy P., *Neither Sharks nor Wolves*, Chatham Publishing, London, 1999

Hadley, Michael L., *Count not the Dead; The Popular Image of the German Submarine*, McGill-Queen's University Press, London, 1999

GLOSSARY

A full glossary of terms relevant to the Kriegsmarine would be an exhaustive and massive work in its own right, so this brief coverage will restrict itself to the most commonly encountered terms.

Abteilung Department, section or detachment

Backbord Port

Befehlshaber Commander (*Oberbefehlshaber* Commander in Chief, *Obersten Befehlshaber* Supreme commander)

Begleitschiff Escort ship

Feindfahrt War cruise

Führer (as in e.g. *Führer der Schnellboote*) Flag officer

Hilfskreuzer Auxiliary cruiser, a merchant ship fitted out with disguised weapons usually operating alone against enemy shipping

Kommando Command (*Oberkommando* High command)

Marine A term used to denote navy or naval in general, and not used as in English to denote naval infantry or commando-type troops

Minensuchboot Minesweeper, a large range of ships of different size and class were used for minesweeping duties

Panzerschiff Armoured ship, this term was used to describe the heavily armoured cruisers of the type referred to by the Allies as pocket battleships

Räumboot A small motor minesweeper

Schlachtschiff Battleship, the term was used more widely in German and also encompassed slightly less powerful ships, that would be classed elsewhere as battlecruisers

Schnellboot Fast boat, known to the Allies as E-boats, this was the term used in the German Navy for what would be thought of as a motor torpedo boat, but were much larger than the equivalent Allied boats

Steuerbord Starboard

Torpedoboot Torpedo boat, German Navy torpedo boats were the equivalent to the lighter classes of Allied destroyer escorts

Wasserbomben Depth charges

Werft Shipyard or dockyard (*Marinewerft* Naval Dockyard)

Zerstörer Destroyer, German destroyers in general were much larger than typical Allied vessels of this type

The following selection may give the reader an idea of the sort of traditional links that were formed by the choice of name for some of the Kriegsmarine's warships. Some of the names themselves may be familiar, but the details of the individuals themselves may be less well known.

Bismarck Named for Otto, Fürst von Bismarck (1819–1898), the 'Iron Chancellor', who guided Wilhelm I of Prussia to his position as Kaiser of a united Germany.

Tirpitz Named for Grossadmiral Alfred von Tirpitz (1849–1930), commander-in-chief of the Imperial German Navy.

Scharnhorst Named for Gerhard Johann von Scharnhorst (1755–1813), a visionary social and military reformer responsible for the modernisation of the Prussian Army.

Gneisenau Named for August Wilhelm Anton Graf Neidhardt von Gneisenau (1760–1831), the great Prussian general and military reformer who introduced promotion on merit and abolished corporal punishment and special privileges for those from the higher classes.

Admiral Graf Spee Named for Maximilian Johannes Maria Hubertus, Reichsgraf von Spee (1861–1914), commander of the German East Asia Cruiser Squadron, who went down with his ship after a ferocious battle near the Falkland Islands.

Admiral Scheer Named for Reinhard Scheer (1863–1928), commanding officer of the High Seas Fleet at the Battle of Jutland and strong supporter of U-boat warfare.

Blücher Named for Generalfeldmarschall Gebhard Leberecht Fürst Blücher von Wahlstatt (1742–1819), the hero of Waterloo, whose timely arrival on the battlefield saved Wellington's forces from probable defeat. 'Papa' Blücher was greatly loved by the common soldier of his day.

Admiral Hipper Named for Franz, Ritter von Hipper (1863–1932), one of the fleet's senior commanders during the battle of Jutland who also took a keen interest in the technical development of the torpedo.

Prinz Eugen Named for Prince Eugene of Savoy (1663–1736), an Austrian field marshal who fought in the Liberation Wars against the French.

Hitler was known for his strong dislike of the Prussian Juncker traditions, so much so that when the Order of the Iron Cross was reinstituted in 1939, he refused to countenance holders of the Knight's Cross being referred to as 'Knights' of the Order, because it smacked too much of Juncker terminology. Winners were to be known as 'Bearers' of the Order. Bearing in mind the Navy's strong tendency to avoid political indoctrination and National Socialist ideology wherever possible, it is interesting that all of the major units of the Kriegsmarine were named after German heroes who upheld the noblest of Prussian traditions that Hitler seemed to detest so much.

COLOUR PLATE COMMENTARY

A: THE NEW RECRUIT

This plate shows our newly trained recruit. He has just completed his basic training with 1 Schiffssstammabteilung der Ostsee, the First Reserve Detachment of the Baltic Fleet, based in Kiel. Not yet allocated to a ship, he still wears the cap ribbon of his particular sailor's pool. As shown, he wears the basic service dress of all lower-ranked sailors, the traditional 'square rig'. Cut from good-quality blue wool, it was a warm and functional form of dress as well as reflecting long-standing naval tradition. Apart from the addition of the National Socialist emblem on the left breast it is very similar to its Imperial predecessor. His cap was provided with both blue and white covers for winter and summer wear.

The sailor's collar (1), known as the *Kieler Kragen*, was cut from cotton material. The interior bib portion was in plain undyed material and had two long laces for tying around the wearer's chest. This was attached in place before the woollen pullover shirt was put on. The exterior flap, which passed through the wide neck hole of the pullover and lay over the pullover's own integral wool collar flap, was in contrasting cornflower blue. The design was borrowed from that worn by the Royal Navy, the three white border lines said to commemorate Nelson's three great naval victories.

At the neck, a traditional sailor's black silk neckerchief (2) is worn. This is a square of black silk fabric with a single blue line woven through it. It is first folded in half, diagonally, then folded over repeatedly to form a long strip of material that, when tied in the manner shown, produces the correct neckerchief form. The ensemble is finished off with a bow of white lace. Although many sailors contrived to produce ready-tied neckerchiefs that could simply be put on over the head when needed, many ship's captains insisted that the sailor tie his neckerchief anew, each time it was put on.

The cap ribbon on the sailor's cap (3) also had to be attached in a certain fashion. At each side of the cap was a vertical cord thread. At the rear were two more, with two further threads at 45 degree angles. The cap ribbon was placed on the cap, the mid portion of the lettering centred on the front of the cap, between two beads of wool piping and passed through the two cords at the side, around the cap and under the vertical and slanted cords at the rear. It was then brought back and tucked under the slanted cord, and the remaining length left to hang loose. As the ends of the ribbon were cut at 45 degree angles, this resulted in the loose ends forming a swallowtail effect. The ribbons were never to be simply tied in a knot at the rear of the cap.

Also shown are two of the most common forms of life vest issued to Kriegsmarine sailors. At its simplest, this consisted of a strip of fabric tied around the chest (4). Small vertical compartments sewn into the vest were filled with kapok flotation material. Others, like the second example shown (5), were more elaborate and featured inflatable panels and collars. These were fitted with their own oxygen cylinder for rapid inflation and also had a small mouthpiece so they could be inflated manually.

Illustrated are some of the issues of personal kit provided to sailors, including warm woollen underwear (6), leather ankle boots (7) and canvas shoes (8), combination knife-and-fork eating utensil (9) and wrist watch (10) – note the Navy issue mark KM on the dial. Raincoats (11) were also provided to NCOs and officers. These were double breasted and cut like the greatcoat, but in waterproofed material with a dark-blue woollen collar.

Also illustrated is the sailor's personal ID tag (12), with the inscription 'Kriegsmarine', followed by his personal number, year of enrolment, and code letter indicating his career grouping. This was worn around the neck on a cord or metal chain. Also shown is the standard naval belt buckle (13) in gilded light metal alloy, and the naval issue bosun's whistle (14).

B: TRAINING

All Kriegsmarine sailors, of whatever rank, had to prove themselves first as competent soldiers. In fact, the German fashion was to refer to all servicemen as soldiers, whether they served on land, sea or in the air. Though the basic infantry training they undertook was less extensive than that given to Army soldiers, it provided the sailor with all the basic military skills including drill movements, combat skills, self reliance and, most importantly, discipline.

View (1) shows a sailor in field grey dress being given instruction on the firing range. He wears the standard M35 steel helmet as issued to the Army (but with the naval version of the national emblem worn as a decal on the left side), and is using the Kar98k rifle, the basic weapon of the German Army, with accompanying leather ammo pouches and braces. The dress worn by this recruit is the drill uniform. This lacks the pockets found on the normal field grey uniform. The officer instructing the recruit is in the field grey service uniform used whilst in training, and also by naval land units such as coastal artillery, naval infantry, etc. His cap is also in field grey rather than dark blue. Although this uniform is very similar to that of the Army, there are numerous subtle design differences that set it apart.

View (2) shows a sailor being put through his paces on the training grounds. In full combat kit with rifle and steel helmet, he is toiling to keep the pace required by his NCO. The NCO, in normal service dress and field cap, runs alongside him shouting such encouragement (or abuse) as is required to motivate the recruit. This is almost certainly not what the recruit thought being a sailor was all about!

View (3) shows another important part of basic training – discipline. This miserable sailor, with his filthy drill uniform and mud-spattered face, has obviously not performed to the required standard. He stands ramrod straight, feet together, at attention. Note the manner in which the hands are held to the seam of the trouser leg, with the arms slightly bent, quite different to the British or American style.

The senior warrant officer bawling him out is resplendent in his full service dress with polished jackboots and peaked service cap. The rings on his sleeve indicate his position as *Der Spiess*, or senior NCO of the training establishment. This was a position, not a rank, and those appointed could range from a relatively junior sergeant to a senior warrant officer, the point being that they are the most senior NCO of that unit or establishment.

The Kriegsmarine was very 'professional', with a much higher level of technical specialists within its ranks than most of the other services. In most cases, sailors worked as part of a small team that depended on every man pulling his weight and supporting his comrades. One poor sailor could spell disaster in certain cases, submarine crews being the most obvious example. It was extremely important that recruits learned discipline, not only the discipline that required an instant response to a superior's orders, but also the self-discipline which is needed for effective teamwork. NCO candidates would often return to this sort of training later in their careers, but to learn to give effective commands rather than receive them.

C: MAINTENANCE

Having completed his training and joined the active reserve sailor's pool of the North Sea Fleet, this sailor has eventually been posted to his first ship. In this case it is one of the older, coal-power coastal minesweepers. One of the great problems with coal-powered ships was that eventually they required to be refuelled, which invariably meant a spell of absolutely filthy and back-breaking physical labour, re-filling the ship's bunkers with ton upon ton of coal (1). During this exercise, the crewmen would become filthy, looking more like chimney sweeps than sailors. Not only the crew, but the ship, too, would acquire a coating of black coal dust, so that once the job was complete the sailors faced even more hard, physical labour in returning the ship to a spick and span state before they could think of doing the same for themselves.

As the war progressed, however, and oil shortages began to bite, these older coal-powered vessels proved their worth and gave sterling service.

The crewmen are wearing the white moleskin working uniforms. Though it may seem perverse that sailors involved in the filthiest of duties were given white working uniforms, they cleaned up well, the cleaning itself giving sailors with idle hands something else to do – these smaller coastal vessels could not boast the on-board laundries of the larger capital ships.

Cleaning and maintenance work were a perennial part of a sailor's life, whether it was coaling on small ships such as this minesweeper, refreshing well-worn paintwork on the hull of an ocean-going destroyer (2), or swabbing the decks of a cruiser (3). Later in the war, freshening up pale-grey paintwork on the superstructure or polishing brasswork would be replaced by painting drab, disruptive camouflage schemes on visible surfaces to confuse the enemy, but a sailor's life would rarely be free of such tedious tasks.

D: NAVAL FLAK GUNS

This plate shows the various members of the gunnery team on the heavy, twin 10.5 cm flak gun of a major warship such as a heavy cruiser or battleship. The central illustration (1), shows the gun crew servicing the heavy flak guns, wearing steel helmets and life jackets. Occasionally, gun crews would wear the full leather jacket and trousers outfits designed for wear by engine-room personnel and also standard issue to U-boat crews. These weapons were fitted to most of the larger German warships including battleships, battlecruisers, pocket battleships and heavy cruisers. Inset (2), shows the control position for the flak guns, consisting of a large binocular sighting mechanism within an armoured

sphere. As well as the sights for the optics, the position contained the gunnery control equipment that passed range and trajectory setting to the guns. Although German ship-mounted radar was inferior to that fitted to British ships, their optical range-finding mechanisms were superb. A hatch was fitted to the top of the housing, where one of the crew, wearing his communication headset (3), can be seen.

In large warships such as the *Bismarck*, an amazingly high rate of fire could be achieved despite the massive effort required to move the heavy shells manually from the shell lockers, as shown (4), to the turret and to load them into the breech. An experienced team of gunners, working like a smooth, well-oiled machine, could fire off two to three salvos per minute.

E: THE S-BOAT IN ACTION

The action scene shows a late-model S-boat in action against shipping in the English Channel during 1944. Moving at high speed towards its target, it has just launched two of its complement of four 21-inch torpedoes. Immediately after firing the torpedoes, the S-boat would break off and use its extremely high speed of up to 40 knots to avoid return fire from its target or any escort vessels.

Although comparatively heavily armed and very fast and agile, S-boats had very little protection against enemy gunfire of anything other than fairly light calibre, and depended on that speed and agility to keep them out of harm's way. Later, improved versions as shown here had an armoured wheelhouse/bridge area that provided a modicum of protection.

Here, the S-boat has come under attack from an escorting fighter-bomber and is using its quad 2 cm *flakvierling* gun in a defensive role. This excellent weapon could also be used in an anti-shipping role against unarmoured merchant vessels, or against enemy MTBs, a foe that the S-boats regularly encountered in their forays into the Channel.

As well as attacking shipping with their torpedoes, S-boats carried out many successful mine-laying sorties along the English coast.

F: THE AUXILIARY CRUISER

One of the most unusual forms of service in the Navy was with the auxiliary cruisers. These were former merchant ships that were converted in considerable secrecy to give them a formidable array of concealed weapons that allowed them to take on and defeat an armed merchantman or even smaller warships, although in most cases they were dangerously outgunned if they met a large enemy warship. These vessels carried 5.9-inch guns, flak guns, torpedoes and even their own floatplanes for reconnaissance work. Although all but one were eventually tracked down and sunk by the Allied navies, they caused considerable disruption to Allied shipping and sunk a total of 102 enemy ships, representing some 664,630 tons, including one medium cruiser.

Those serving on these vessels reported to their ships in civilian clothes in order to disguise their real nature, and on returning to port left their ship in the same manner. Great effort went into design work to ensure that gun barrels resembled crane derricks, turrets resembled large cable reels, seaplanes were stored in the hold with wings folded or removed, and torpedo tubes were below the waterline. The success with which such measures were taken is reflected by the number of successful attacks that were made on unsuspecting Allied ships, which allowed the auxiliary cruisers to draw too close before trying to escape or raising an alarm until too late.

In this plate we see *Schiff 16*, the *Atlantis*. In the first view **(1)** we see her as an innocent merchantman, the Japanese *Kasil Maru*, and painted in the correct colours for the Japanese ship, during the *Atlantis'* first cruise in 1940. At this point in the war, Japan was still a neutral country. Often, a few crewmen would put on female attire over their normal dress and perhaps appear on deck with an (empty) pram. From a distance, viewed through binoculars from the intended victim, it would appear that civilians were on board, so this could not of course be a warship. One ruse used was to wear the sailor's cap, with ribbon turned inside out so that the mirror image resembled Cyrillic script, with a red star pinned above, and 'Hey Presto', our Kriegsmarine sailor **(2)** became a Soviet seaman. The disguises may have been crude, but when it is borne in mind they would be observed from far off through binoculars, they were very effective.

On attacking, the disguises would be cast aside, guns revealed and the Reichskriegsflagge run up the mast. The auxiliary cruiser would then go into action as a legitimate warship. A warning shot would be fired with a demand to stop. If this failed, the next shot would be aimed at the enemy ship's radio room to prevent a warning or distress message being sent, or to halt any signals already in progress.

If the victim were carrying a strategically valuable cargo, a prize crew would be put on board to attempt to run the captured ship through the British blockade and back to Germany. If the cargo did not warrant such a measure, the enemy ship would be sunk, and her crew and any passengers taken aboard the auxiliary cruiser – unless close to land, in which case they would be given directions to the nearest landfall.

The second view shows our auxiliary cruiser with her true colours revealed **(3)**. The enemy merchantman had attempted to send an 'RRRRR . . .' signal indicating attack by an enemy surface raider, and so her radio room has been shelled and is now ablaze. The *Atlantis'* main armament was concealed behind movable panels in the ship's upper hull sides. These, though large, were cleverly counterbalanced with weights making them quick and easy to move. It is estimated that these panels could be moved and the gun turrets traversed into action stations in just a few seconds. Guns not concealed behind movable panels were often disguised as innocent objects, such as cable drums. The example shown here is of the type used on the *Widder*, Ship 21 **(4)**.

Overhead, the raider's Arado 196 floatplane keeps a wary eye on the horizon in case any enemy vessels have intercepted the merchantman's warning signal and attempt to intervene. The seaplane was not catapult launched as on a normal warship, but was stored in the hold with its wings removed. The plane had to be hoisted out of the hold on to the hatch cover, assembled, then lowered by crane into the water and thus could only be used in calm conditions.

Auxiliary cruisers such as the *Atlantis* gained a reputation for treating their captives with great chivalry.

G: MINIATURE SUBMARINES

This plate shows one of the one-man torpedo devices used by the KM in the latter part of the war. The painted insignia just below the cockpit is for K-Flot Number 1. This version, the *Neger*, was the original type. Almost as dangerous to their operators as to the enemy, these weapons achieved little in the way of success. The small plexiglass dome was only intended to provide a measure of protection against spray and flooding. The *Neger* had no diving capability and the later improved version, the *Marder*, could only dive to a very limited depth.

One can only imagine the intense discomfort of sitting in such a terribly cramped cockpit, in freezing cold temperatures, in stale air requiring breathing apparatus, battered by the waves and liable to be spotted by the enemy at any time. With no diving capability and no form of defensive armament, the *Neger* was all but doomed once spotted. Indeed, two-thirds of *Neger* operators who set off on operations never returned.

The *Marder/Neger* operator wore warm woollen underclothes over which he donned either a rubberised frogman type suit, or more often, a simple one-piece denim boiler suit type overall **(2)**. A cloth helmet **(3)** was worn, attached by straps, along with goggles **(4)** and an oxygen mask linked to a basic oxygen supply as used on aircraft. A *Tauchretter* **(5)** escape apparatus, of the type used on submarines, was also provided. The oxygen mask was not intended for breathing underwater, but for allowing the operator to breathe more easily in the stale air of the cramped cockpit.

The helmet, overalls and breathing apparatus are shown in the detail view **(6)**. An overall view of the *Neger*, showing how its torpedo was slung under the *Neger* itself, is provided at **(1)**. The projecting spike in front of the cockpit cover is a simple aiming device. The entire vessel would be aimed at its target before releasing the torpedo slung below. The two loops added along the spine of the *Neger* are for attaching cables to lift the vessel in or out of the water. Initially, the *Neger* had to be physically manhandled into the water by a large team of men, but ultimately a wheeled beaching trolley of the type shown was provided.

No insignia were worn by *Marder/Neger* operators on the overalls worn on active service, but a range of cloth insignia as shown at **(7)** was produced for wear on the blue service uniform. The insignia consisted of a sawfish over a rope circle, with one, two or three Swords added to indicate a total of 1, 2 or 3 missions undertaken. A metal clasp **(8)** was also planned but never put into volume production though some were awarded 'on paper'. Given the high attrition rate for men serving in the K-Verbände, only a few lived long enough to earn any other than the lowest grades.

H: LAND-BASED NAVAL SERVICE

Towards the end of the war, large numbers of surplus sailors, men who had been fully trained, but for whom, due to combat losses, there were no longer any ships or submarines on which to serve, were transferred to infantry units.

These men had already had an element of basic infantry training during their recruit days, and so were given only a few rushed days of refresher training in the latest combat techniques and new weapons, such as the *Panzerfaust*, before being rushed into action. This group of sailors has been formed into a tank-hunting team and sent into action near Hamburg in the closing days of the war. Though they have scored several successes, their efforts were far too late to do anything other than delay their surrender by a few days. This team has just surrendered to a British unit. One sailor is being questioned by a British military policeman, who is thumbing through the sailor's identity document, the *Soldbuch*.

The sailor has come a long way from his early days as a freshly trained recruit, resplendent in his blue naval uniform. Late-war combat clothing used material of very poor quality, much of its wool content being replaced by shoddy waste material. These uniforms looked shabby, and as soon as they became wet, lost much of whatever shaping they had. They had poor insulation qualities, too, and in cold climes gave little thermal protection. The shiny jackboots of the early years were replaced by short ankle boots and canvas gaiters, and the early leather belts and braces by cheap webbing straps. The steel helmet had also been simplified, the neatly rolled edge of the early 1935 pattern replaced by a raw unfinished cut on the 1942 pattern. Decals are no longer used. The Iron Cross ribbon in his buttonhole and the

Wound Badge and Fleet War Badge on his left breast pocket, however, identify him as veteran with combat service in his 'old' role as a sailor.

One thing that had not deteriorated was the quality of his weapon. He has just surrendered his MP40 machine pistol, still one of the best automatic weapons in use. The rest of the squad have surrendered their *Panzerfausten*, excellent single-shot anti-tank weapons, which lie in a pile alongside their discarded rifles. Even where poorer quality materials have been used, such as the laminated rather than solid wood stocks on the rifle, or the dull grey chemical finish to the metalwork instead of fine gun-bluing, the weapons themselves remained highly effective.

This soldier/sailor has probably not slept or eaten for the last few chaotic days of the war and, red eyed and unshaven, he looks on the edge of exhaustion. His interrogation is watched by his squad commander, a junior officer who wears a bizarre combination of whatever clothing was available. In his case, this is a mixture of army field grey trousers and ankle boots, a Luftwaffe camouflaged ground troop jacket and his old blue naval officer's cap. The latter was probably retained as its gold-braid-edged peak instantly identified him as an officer to the rest of the hastily thrown together squad.

COMPANION SERIES FROM OSPREY

ESSENTIAL HISTORIES
Concise studies of the motives, methods and repercussions of human conflict, spanning history from ancient times to the present day. Each volume studies one major war or arena of war, providing an indispensable guide to the fighting itself, the people involved, and its lasting impact on the world around it.

MEN-AT-ARMS
The uniforms, equipment, insignia, history and organisation of the world's military forces from earliest times to the present day. Authoritative text and full-colour artwork, photographs and diagrams bring over 5000 years of history vividly to life.

ELITE
This series focuses on uniforms, equipment, insignia and unit histories in the same way as Men-at-Arms but in more extended treatments of larger subjects, also including personalities and techniques of warfare.

NEW VANGUARD
The design, development, operation and history of the machinery of warfare through the ages. Photographs, full-colour artwork and cutaway drawings support detailed examinations of the most significant mechanical innovations in the history of human conflict.

ORDER OF BATTLE
The greatest battles in history, featuring unit-by-unit examinations of the troops and their movements as well as analysis of the commanders' original objectives and actual achievements. Colour maps including a large fold-out base map, organisational diagrams and photographs help the reader to trace the course of the fighting in unprecedented detail.

CAMPAIGN
Accounts of history's greatest conflicts, detailing the command strategies, tactics, movements and actions of the opposing forces throughout the crucial stages of each campaign. Full-colour battle scenes, 3-dimensional 'bird's-eye views', photographs and battle maps guide the reader through each engagement from its origins to its conclusion.

AIRCRAFT OF THE ACES
Portraits of the elite pilots of the 20th century's major air campaigns, including unique interviews with surviving aces. Unit listings, scale plans and full-colour artwork combine with the best archival photography available to provide a detailed insight into the experience of war in the air.

COMBAT AIRCRAFT
The world's greatest military aircraft and combat units and their crews, examined in detail. Each exploration of the leading technology, men and machines of aviation history is supported by unit listings and other data, artwork, scale plans, and archival photography.

INDEX